RAND NATIONAL DEFENSE RESEARCH INSTITUTE

From Patchwork to Framework

A Review of Title 10 Authorities for Security Cooperation

David E. Thaler, Michael J. McNerney, Beth Grill,
Jefferson P. Marquis, Amanda Kadlec

Prepared for the Office of the Secretary of Defense

For more information on this publication, visit www.rand.org/t/RR1438

Library of Congress Cataloging-in-Publication Data is available for this publication.
ISBN: 978-0-8330-9408-7

Published by the RAND Corporation, Santa Monica, Calif.
© Copyright 2016 RAND Corporation
RAND® is a registered trademark.

Support RAND
Make a tax-deductible charitable contribution at
www.rand.org/giving/contribute

www.rand.org

Preface

U.S. efforts to build the capacity of foreign partners have a long history. The United States exported arms to allies during World War I, enacted the Lend Lease Act in 1941, and cooperated with security forces around the world to counter the expansion of communism during the Cold War and strengthen democratic principles after communism's collapse. While Department of Defense (DoD) efforts in security cooperation had been evolving to meet a changing post–Cold War global security environment, building partner capacity gained new impetus in U.S. national strategy after the terrorist attacks against the United States on September 11, 2001. However, the accelerated proliferation of legislative authorities for the DoD in Public Law and Title 10 of the U.S. Code in the ensuing 15 years has created an increasingly unwieldy catalog of statutes, which has generated severe challenges in planning and execution of security cooperation with foreign partners. The large set of authorities used for security cooperation has become known as a "patchwork" because of the need to patch together multiple authorities and associated yet unsynchronized processes, resources, programs, and organizations to execute individual initiatives with partner nations.

This report develops a framework and options to streamline the patchwork of authorities for security cooperation that DoD—including the Office of the Secretary of Defense, the Joint Staff, the combatant commands, the military services, and defense agencies—employs. The objective is to frame Title 10 security cooperation authorities in a holistic, logical way, identify redundancies and gaps, and offer recommendations for changes in authorities that reduce the complexities involved in implementation, making it easier for DoD's security cooperation workforce to use them to work with partner nations in support of U.S. national security strategy.

This research should be of interest to those in the executive and legislative branches, as well as outside analysts involved with the statutory bases of security cooperation.

This research was sponsored by the Office of the Secretary of Defense and conducted within the International Security and Defense Policy Center of the RAND National Defense Research Institute, a federally funded research and development center sponsored by the Office of the Secretary of Defense, the Joint Staff, the Unified Combatant Commands, the Navy, the Marine Corps, the defense agencies, and the defense Intelligence Community.

For more information on the International Security and Defense Policy Center, see www.rand.org/nsrd/ndri/centers/isdp or contact the director (contact information is provided on the web page).

Contents

Figures and Tables

Figures

Tables

Summary

The United States cooperates with governments around the world in support of common security interests. U.S. strategy assumes a reliance on foreign partners to play a role in providing security. U.S. security cooperation efforts help them do this—thus, they are fundamental to implementing foreign policy and national security strategies. The Department of Defense (DoD) plays a crucial role in these efforts, conducting thousands of security cooperation activities each year ranging from multiservice military exercises to chaplain exchanges and everything in between. Each of these activities must fit within a set of parameters authorized by Congress. These authorities provide the legal basis by which the U.S. government can educate, train, equip, and exercise with foreign security forces and institutions and conduct information-sharing activities. The United States pursues these efforts to strengthen its relationships with these countries and build their capacity to operate alongside or instead of U.S. military forces. Many of these authorities are codified in Title 22 of the U.S. Code, which directs U.S. foreign assistance.[1] At least since the end of the Cold War, security cooperation authorities codified in Title 10, which directs the armed forces, have grown as new expectations for DoD efforts in this realm required greater flexibility and agility in addressing threats to U.S. interests. This expansion process of Title 10 authorities was vastly accelerated after the terrorist attacks of September 11, 2001.

---

[1] The U.S. government defines foreign assistance as "aid given by the United States to other countries to support global peace, security, and development efforts, and provide humanitarian relief during times of crisis." Foreign Assistance Dashboard, "What Is U.S. Government Foreign Assistance," United States government, web page, undated.

In the past 15 years, Title 10 authorities governing security cooperation have been added and adjusted every year, strengthening the
ability of DoD to cooperate with foreign partners. As just one example, the Coalition Readiness Support Program, authorized through a
number of Title 10 statutes and Public Laws, enabled DoD to quickly
train and equip less-capable partners to operate alongside U.S. forces
in Afghanistan.

As might be expected when fighting two wars and dramatically
expanding its counterterrorism mission, DoD's proposals to Congress
for new and revised authorities since 2001 have been voluminous and
ad hoc. Despite a clear process for submitting legislative proposals, these
rapid changes in the security environment made it challenging for both
DoD and Congress to maintain a strategic, deliberative approach. To
further complicate matters, after a decade of focusing on counterinsurgency and counterterrorism operations, DoD is trying to adjust to a
range of newly emerging threats in such areas as cyber warfare, space-
based capabilities, and maritime security.

Building on its past research on this topic, RAND identified 123
Title 10 authorities—106 "core" statutes that directly authorize activities and 17 "supporting" ones that legislate transfer of funds or mandate reports to Congress—in 2016 that were relevant to security cooperation. This rapid, piecemeal growth has resulted in an increasingly
unwieldy patchwork of statutes that contain redundancies, limitations,
gaps, and expanding demands on DoD staffers who must justify every
activity with foreign partners under one of these authorities. These staff
members must navigate their way not only through multiple authorities but also associated and unsynchronized processes, resources, programs, and organizations to execute individual initiatives with partner
nations. At the other end of this process, members of Congress and
their staffs struggle to place all these activities in the context of a coherent strategy, while providing guidance and oversight. As a result, major
inefficiencies have developed in planning, executing, and overseeing
security cooperation activities; arguably, some efforts have been less
effective than they could be. As defense headquarter staffs shrink and
planning grows increasingly complex, the risk of canceled or ineffective
events has grown significantly. Moreover, policymakers and congres-

sional staff face growing challenges providing guidance and oversight and evaluating progress toward larger objectives.

In this report, we attempt to answer the following questions:

- What challenges does the "patchwork" of Title 10 security cooperation authorities present to security cooperation personnel in DoD and their congressional overseers?
- How should these authorities be framed to better rationalize how DoD approaches Congress for legislation to conduct security cooperation?
- Within this framework, what revisions to existing authorities will enable DoD to address the challenges identified, reduce overlap, fill gaps, and simplify the patchwork?

As described in Chapter One, we approached our research through several steps. We started with a review of existing research within and outside of RAND. An important part of this past work was a catalog of security cooperation authorities RAND developed in 2010, which the team updated by reviewing Public Laws and National Defense Authorization Acts in 2012 and 2015. This provided a baseline of existing authorities as of fiscal year 2016. The team then organized several focused discussion sessions with officials involved in security cooperation from DoD and Congress, culminating in a RAND-led workshop on Capitol Hill. These discussions elicited important insights about the challenges of security cooperation authorities and opportunities for shifting from a patchwork to a more structured framework. Drawing from these insights, we designed a framework that categorizes Title 10 security cooperation authorities and puts them in the context of the various objectives and approaches DoD was pursuing. Using that framework, the team analyzed these authorities and suggested ways to consolidate, revise, and add to them.

Challenges the Existing Title 10 Authorities Present

In Chapter Two, we focus on the first research question: What challenges does DoD's patchwork of security cooperation authorities present? DoD staff involved in security cooperation identified three basic areas of concern.

First, the proliferation and complexity of authorities make it difficult to develop security cooperation initiatives with partners, especially ambitious efforts that integrate several types of activities requiring multiple authorities. Every authority details different requirements and constraints concerning which partners are eligible, under what circumstances, and with what reporting requirements. Military planners in the field often have little experience managing security cooperation and rotate every two to three years, while more experienced DoD civilians are few in number with perhaps a handful to support a combatant command. Many initiatives require several authorities using different sources of funding on different cycles with different processes and restrictions, and different congressional reporting requirements. Should funding for one of these authorities fall through, major events may be canceled or radically restructured. Despite its value in helping deploy partners to Afghanistan, the Coalition Readiness Support Program example discussed earlier provided only one of the five authorities necessary to support four infantry battalions from the country of Georgia. Similarly, it was one of only six authorities required to loan Mine Resistant Ambush Protected vehicles to another country. In addition to the inefficiencies created by this patchwork approach, the delays and changes that result from associated planning problems can generate confusion with partners and setbacks in strengthening relationships and building a partner's capabilities. Even more-modest efforts can require multiple authorities, leading some planners to avoid smaller programs because they may only have time for one or two high-visibility efforts. Finally, greater complexity has required greater involvement by DoD lawyers to interpret what is and is not allowed, with different interpretations by different individuals or organizations or at different times. For example, can a particular maritime training event be considered a counterterrorism effort? Can a particular exercise pay for certain civilians to attend? Legal uncertainties like these have resulted in delays and cancellations, generating further frustration and confusion between U.S. and foreign military planners.

Second, many DoD staff whom we engaged noted that they plan with a five-year time horizon but are funded in only one- or two-year increments. Thus, planning involves a significant amount of guesswork, and programs can become episodic and unsustainable, for example, when funding is increased one year then reduced unexpectedly the next. This then undermines the ability of partners to program funds for equipment sustainment and follow-on training. In addition, when a program is approved late in a fiscal year, there are sometimes only weeks available to obligate funds before funds expire. The slightest complication can result in cancellation of an activity. If training in a particular fiscal year is dependent on the timely provision of equipment, procurement delays can then derail planned training, potentially undermining the entire effort. Most DoD staff recognized that one-year funding can create a healthy sense of focus and urgency, but some suggested that two-year and multiyear funding could maintain the necessary urgency through effective oversight, including through a continued requirement for annual justifications and reporting to Congress.

Third, as DoD shifts from a counterinsurgency and counterterrorism focus to an emphasis on a wider array of emerging threats, gaps in authorities are becoming more evident. In some cases, planners try to game the system, stretching the limits of what an authority might allow. In other cases, military leaders simply do not pursue their top priority activity. For example, planners have sometimes emphasized the counterterrorism benefits of an activity when the focus is really on cybersecurity. Or planners emphasize the counternarcotics benefits of maritime security efforts when the focus is at least as much on monitoring Chinese activity in the South China Sea. In the case of ballistic missile defense, Congress has emphasized the importance of regional cooperation to counter missile threats from North Korea and Iran, but DoD has limited or unclear authorities on this issue. Aspects of intelligence sharing, defense institution building, countering extremism, strengthening resilience against hybrid warfare threats, and sustainment of partner equipment are other areas with potentially insufficiently flexible authorities. It also can be challenging for DoD to work with interior agencies or other civilian authorities to help address these emerging threats or to work with regional organizations rather than just bilaterally with national governments. Finally, despite improvements in its ability to deliver equipment quickly to partners, particularly for counterterrorism objectives, there may be opportunities for authorities that allow DoD to accelerate its assistance efforts.

Congressional Perspectives

As we discuss at the end of Chapter Two, although congressional staff we engaged agree that authorities have become more of a patchwork and there are opportunities for improvement that Congress could consider, many point out that there are several factors that complicate efforts to simplify legislative authorities. First, these staffers argue that DoD's internal processes and bureaucracy create even greater challenges than the authorities themselves. How many of the complaints about delays and gaming the system might be resolved through improved DoD organization, planning, and training? Second, DoD requests and reporting tend to focus on equipment or tactical objectives and rarely explain the linkages to broader strategies. How do these various activities aggregate within a coherent, detailed plan? What are the concrete intended effects of these efforts, and how does DoD measure progress?

Perhaps most important, though, is the fact that Congress has a legitimate oversight responsibility that requires visibility over these activities and some level of control to ensure the intent of Congress is followed when expending taxpayer dollars. Restrictions exist for important reasons, for example, to avoid overly militarizing U.S. foreign policy; reduce human rights abuses; reduce waste; and prevent fraud. Narrower authorities are easier for busy members of Congress and their small staffs to examine and manage. Some members of Congress have a particular interest in a security cooperation program and may be less supportive of more generic legislation.

Congressional staffers we engaged also largely agreed that emerging security challenges mean that a focus on counterterrorism cannot come at the expense of other strategic concerns, many of which are related to Russian and Chinese capabilities and actions. Improvements

in authorities should help DoD balance requirements for building partner capabilities in such areas as counterterrorism with requirements to
build major combat capabilities.

One approach that seemed to have some staff support was to
tackle these challenges in multiple steps, starting with proposals to
consolidate authorities that serve similar purposes, e.g., education.
Careful consolidations of more complex authorities could follow. We
discuss these issues in greater detail in Chapter Two.

Designing a Framework

In Chapter Three, we focus on our second research question: How
should these authorities be framed to better rationalize how DoD
approaches Congress for legislation to conduct security cooperation?
To start, we describe several options for categorizing security cooperation authorities, based on the different ways DoD planners already
classify the basic components of security cooperation. In general, planners organize security cooperation around ends (objectives), ways (missions), or means (activities). Each approach captures some but not all
conditions under which various security cooperation resources may
apply. After analyzing the pros and cons of each approach, we settle
on a hybrid approach that we contend most effectively organizes and
rationalizes the existing patchwork.

The starting point for the framework is an activity-based category, which incorporates many of the authorities that enable standard, enduring security cooperation tasks, such as train-and-equip,
education, and exercises. Two additional categories capture the different ways other authorities are specialized. Our mission-based category focuses on some of the purposes for which security cooperation
is authorized, such as counterterrorism, counternarcotics, or maritime
security. Our partner-based category focuses on authorities that specify
cooperation with particular countries or multilateral organizations like
NATO. Drawing on our discussions with practitioners and analysis
of existing and proposed legislation, we organize eight subcategories
under the activity category and seven under mission. Because they are

country specific and limited in number, the partner category has no subcategories. We list existing Title 10 security cooperation authorities under these categories and subcategories in Appendix A.

In addition to helping stakeholders put these authorities in a clearer context, the framework provides the foundation for our team to analyze authorities that may be obsolete, redundant, or in need of modification, as well as potential gaps.

Rationalizing the Patchwork

In Chapter Four, we address our final research question: Within this framework, what revisions to existing authorities will enable DoD to address the challenges identified, reduce overlap, fill gaps, and simplify the patchwork?

By analyzing existing authorities through this framework, the team found options to reduce the overall number of "core" authorities by 15, going from 106 to 91. We suggest revisions and clarifications to a number of authorities and the creation of one new one.

Most of the significant consolidations, revisions, and clarifications we propose fall within the category of standardized, activity-based authorities, which involve routine interactions with foreign forces. For example, we propose consolidating nine authorities facilitating military-to-military engagements into four. We also analyzed 23 authorities facilitating foreign attendance in U.S. military education and technical training programs. We proposed leaving 12 of these authorities as is, consolidating ten others down to two, and broadening the authorization for the Regional Defense Combating Terrorism Fellowship Program to address additional emerging threats, such as cyberattacks.

For mission-based authorities, we propose better aligning six authorities addressing DoD provision of humanitarian assistance overseas. We propose a new authority to facilitate ballistic missile defense training and exercises with advanced partners and expanding a maritime security authority to allow global engagement and capacity building in this mission area. Finally, we propose broadening a cybersecurity authority to allow exchanges of military personnel and limited training and equipment to both military and non-military foreign personnel and to clarify what specific cyber capabilities could be shared with particular types of partners.

We do not recommend any changes to partner-based authorities, because they are intended to be short-term measures focused on particular sets of countries. However, we do recommend migrating the activities associated with these authorities to other categories of standardized activities as soon as (1) near-term U.S. objectives are achieved; (2) motivating circumstances change; or (3) security cooperation activities with those partners normalize. Making such determinations will require regular, analysis-based discussions between DoD and congressional leaders and their staffs.

Appendix B lists the proposed changes to authorities within each category.

Implications of Our Research

It is important to emphasize that this report by no means provides the final answers on how to change current authorities. Several experts emphasized to the study team that potential changes to authorities "do no harm," arguing that DoD staff have applied these authorities to achieve DoD objectives in a timely fashion. Instead, this framework and our proposals are intended to serve as a means to facilitate analysis-based discussions within and among officials from DoD, the Department of State, Congress, and other security cooperation stakeholders.

The insights in this report should help reduce some of the complexity, uncertainty, and gaps in DoD's security cooperation community, while also taking into consideration congressional concerns. In particular, we see four potential benefits from our research. First, our revisions and new authorities should provide greater flexibility to counter hybrid warfare strategies and other emerging threats. Second, our framework should help DoD staff identify and understand existing Title 10 authorities. This will help them use the authorities to plan and execute security cooperation activities, and help policymakers track and shape proposals for future changes. Third, our proposed consolidations and revisions should reduce complexity and thereby improve efficiency and minimize failed planning efforts. Fourth, some of our recommendations should enhance predictability, facilitate the obligation of funds, and align funding with the provision of training and equipment to partners.

Our recommendations can be seen as consistent with and supporting implementation of Presidential Policy Directive 23, "Security Sector Assistance," which mandates that DoD and the Department of State together "continue to implement and refine existing authorities permitting the United States to respond to urgent and emergent priority partner security sector needs…and consider new authorities as necessary."[2] The recommendations can serve as a basis for cooperative improvements in authorities between the departments and between the executive and legislative branches.

Related to this, and looking beyond the research in this report, there remains a need to review DoD and Department of State roles, interests, and coordination processes, as well as analyze what constitutes constructive integration of efforts between Title 10 and Title 22 security cooperation authorities. In addition, DoD will need to complement this analysis of legislative authorities with an evaluation of its own security cooperation planning processes, including how it organizes, how it trains security cooperation professionals, its processes for translating authorities into action, and how it links security cooperation activities to higher-level strategies.

---

[2] The White House, "Presidential Policy Directive/PPD-23: Security Sector Assistance," April 5, 2013, p. 15.

The risks of maintaining the status quo are high. A shrinking force of DoD planners and implementers can no longer absorb inefficiencies from the complexity of security cooperation authorities. This complexity creates confusion internally and with foreign partners, leading to uncertainties, canceled events, and setbacks in relationship-building and capacity-building efforts. It leads to hesitation among planners, who may then propose suboptimal activities that may prove less effective in achieving desired objectives. It impedes the linking of security cooperation activities to resources, plans, and national security objectives. And it makes evaluating progress toward those objectives extremely challenging. Finally, gaps in existing authorities risk tying the hands of DoD staff working with foreign partners to counter emerging threats from Russia, China, North Korea, and Iran, as well as nonstate actors leveraging new capabilities or tactics. Although there is more to do to fully realize a simplified and more-effective system of Title 10 authorities, the framework and analysis in this report should provide a useful step forward.

Acknowledgements

The authors are grateful for the support and help of many individuals. In particular, we would like to thank our sponsor, Deputy Assistant Secretary of Defense for Security Cooperation Tommy Ross, and our point of contact in his office, David Radcliffe, for their insight and guidance during many fruitful interactions. We also greatly appreciate the support of Principal Director Leslie Hunter, who initiated the study and shepherded it through the DoD bureaucracy to ensure its viability.

We are indebted to the officials at the combatant, component, and special operations commands, as well as DoD stakeholders in the Washington, D.C., area, who were so gracious with their time in explaining the challenges they face and in helping us think through ideas for improvement. We also thank the congressional staff members on Capitol Hill who shared their perspectives on sources of these challenges and prospects for change.

Many thanks go to RAND colleague Jennifer Moroney and Wilson Center Global Fellow Jim Schear for their careful, thoughtful reviews of the draft document. Their critiques greatly strengthened this report.

We are further indebted to our RAND colleagues who provided support and advice over the course of this project. Joe Hogler offered his insight to help us conceptualize the process for updating the long list of security cooperation authorities. Walt Perry led discussions with DoD stakeholders in the Washington, D.C., area. And many thanks to Kurt Card, Jayme Fuglesten, and Tim Reggev of RAND's Office of

External Affairs for their extraordinary efforts in setting up congressional staff meetings and arranging and managing a successful workshop on Capitol Hill.

Finally, we appreciate the support of the following colleagues in preparing the draft for review: Francisco Walter, Zack Steinborn, Stephanie Losinger, and Patricia McGarry. We also thank Maria Vega for carefully editing the final draft.

Of course, responsibility for the content of this draft report lies solely with the authors.

CHAPTER ONE

Introduction

President Barack Obama's 2015 National Security Strategy calls for U.S. efforts to prevent conflict by "reaffirming our security commitments to allies and partners, investing in their capabilities to withstand coercion, imposing costs on those who threaten their neighbors or violate fundamental international norms, and embedding our actions within wider regional strategies."[1] The United States seeks to develop and expand partnerships with willing and able nations, regional organizations, and other actors that share common interests in meeting threats to security.

This had been the case since World War II and throughout the Cold War. U.S. Department of Defense (DoD) efforts to work with partners evolved to meet a changing post–Cold War global security environment, but building partner capacity gained new impetus in U.S. national strategy after the terrorist attacks against the United States on September 11, 2001. The United States sought to build coalitions against violent extremist groups and shore up the ability of vulnerable nations to protect their own borders and meet internal threats to stability. Enlisting numerous partners in the fight was seen as a way of minimizing the need for U.S. troops to engage in multiple struggles against these groups. The DoD was at the forefront of these efforts, which centered on rapid provision of operational capabilities to partner nations as well as regional organizations and sub-state actors.

---

[1] The White House, *National Security Strategy*, Washington, D.C., February 2015, p. 10.

But growing complaints from planners and decisionmakers that existing security assistance processes were too slow and unresponsive—and, in some cases, too focused on a few select countries—to meet rapidly evolving threats led the DoD to request additional authorities from Congress that would give the Department more flexibility and agility in building partner capacity. Congress obliged, adding multiple legislative authorities (some requested by the DoD, some initiated by its own members) to Public Law and Title 10 of the U.S. Code that would enable the DoD to quickly and flexibly assist partners. However, the proliferation of such authorities in the ensuing 15 years has created an increasingly unwieldy catalog of statutes that contain redundancies, limitations, gaps, and expanding demands on members of the DoD's security cooperation (SC) workforce who must apply the authorities when working with foreign partners. The set of more than 160 authorities used for SC—in Title 10 (Armed Forces, or DoD), Title 22 (Foreign Relations, or Department of State), other titles in U.S. Code, and numerous Public Laws not codified in U.S. Code, plus some 27 programs created through appropriations or other means—has become known as a "patchwork" because of the need to patch together multiple authorities and associated yet unsynchronized processes, resources, programs, and organizations to execute individual initiatives with partner nations. In an acknowledgment of the need to strengthen the ability of the United States to engage with and build the capacity of its foreign partners, President Obama in 2013 issued "Presidential Policy Directive 23: Security Sector Assistance," which outlined goals and policy guidelines for a new approach to security sector assistance.[2]

In a recent study, *Review of Security Cooperation Mechanisms Combatant Commands Utilize to Build Partner Capacity*, RAND identified and assessed key authorities, programs, processes, resources, and organizational relationships that the U.S. combatant commands (CCMDs) most rely on to build partner capacity (BPC) and achieve high-priority

---

[2]   The White House, "Presidential Policy Directive/PPD-23: Security Sector Assistance," April 5, 2013.

SC objectives.[3] This study found that, for the CCMDs and objectives reviewed, the authorities are adequate for building partner capacity in most cases, but their use in SC planning and execution is exceedingly complex and difficult, leading to substantial inefficiencies and "gaming" of the system to get the job done. Usually, it is left to military personnel in the field who lack necessary experience with SC to figure out how to navigate these complexities, which often differ based on the details of an event being planned.

Moreover, after a decade of counterterrorism (CT) and counterinsurgency operations, newly emerging mission areas (e.g., hybrid warfare, space, maritime security) and modes of cooperation (e.g., regional or multilateral initiatives) have led to suggestions that the authorities be reconfigured accordingly. But DoD's legislative process has not been structured to deal with these issues in a strategic way. Every year, the DoD submits legislative proposals to Congress to request changes in existing authorities for SC and consideration of new authorities. But the rapid changes in the security environment have made it difficult for DoD and Congress to consider proposals in a strategic, deliberative way.

The current report builds upon the earlier study to develop a framework and options to rationalize the patchwork of authorities for SC under Title 10 of the U.S. Code that the DoD—including the Office of the Secretary of Defense (OSD), the Joint Staff, the CCMDs, the Services, and defense agencies—employs. The objective of this report is to frame Title 10 security cooperation authorities in a holistic, logical way, identify redundancies and gaps, and offer recommendations for changes in authorities that reduce the complexities involved in implementation, making it easier for the SC workforce in the DoD to use them to work with partner nations according to U.S. national security strategy. The study underlying this report sought to answer the following questions:

---

[3]   Jennifer D. P. Moroney, David E. Thaler, and Joe Hogler, *Review of Security Cooperation Mechanisms Combatant Commands Utilize to Build Partner Capacity*, Santa Monica, Calif.: RAND Corporation, RR-413-OSD, 2013.

- The patchwork of Title 10 SC authorities presents what challenges to SC personnel in DoD and their congressional overseers?
- How should these authorities be framed to better rationalize how the DoD approaches Congress for legislation to conduct SC?
- Within this framework, what revisions to existing authorities will enable the DoD to address the challenges identified, reduce overlap, fill gaps, and simplify the patchwork?

In answering these questions, the report is not meant to provide the final word on how the SC authorities the DoD uses should be arrayed, but it offers a foundation for discussion and debate in the executive and legislative branches over the statutory bases for U.S. government pursuit of effective partnerships around the world.

Methodology and Organization of the Report

The research in this report builds on previous RAND research to examine the 123 "core" and "supporting" Title 10 statutes that authorize the Secretary of Defense (SecDef) and the DoD to cooperate with foreign partners. These authorities provide an important legal basis by which the DoD can educate, train, equip, and exercise with foreign security forces and institutions and conduct consultative activities, all aimed at improving U.S. relationships with them and building their capacities.

To answer the first question about challenges, the study team held focused discussions with a wide range of DoD and congressional stakeholders to explore their perspectives on Title 10 SC authorities. We identified these stakeholders based on contacts from previous RAND SC-related research, as well as recommendations from our OSD sponsor.[4] These discussions included face-to-face and telephonic interactions with SC personnel in the CCMDs, the military services, OSD, and DoD agencies, and a RAND-led workshop on Capitol Hill among

---

[4] The pool of discussants and organizations we approached was necessarily limited by the scope of our study. While we believe we engaged a good cross-section of DoD SC stakeholders—including many seasoned professionals—we may have omitted challenges and authorities that are important to organizations and individuals we did not engage.

congressional staffers and officials from OSD and the Joint Staff. Chapter Two synthesizes these discussions and provides a summary of the most-common challenges that emerged in planning and executing SC with existing authorities and in overseeing the SC enterprise. The chapter identifies difficulties in using the authorities because of their proliferation and complexity, unpredictability in associated funding, and perceived inflexibility.

In addressing the second question, the team drew from these discussions and from RAND's long experience in SC research to offer a holistic framework in which to organize and rationalize SC authorities. The framework categorizes authorities based on whether they are activity-, mission-, or partner-based. Chapter Three begins with a review of alternative approaches to categorizing authorities and argues for a hybrid option that focuses on their most salient dimensions: activity, mission, or partner. This framework provides a foundation for identifying 1) authorities that may no longer be necessary for achieving SC objectives; 2) redundant, "niche" authorities that potentially could be collapsed into fewer numbers; 3) authorities that may need to be modified; and 4) gaps in authorities that should be bridged to fulfill key SC objectives. In addition, SC planners can use the framework to quickly recognize possible key authorities to execute SC initiatives with partners.

The study team scoured more-recent Public Laws and National Defense Authorization Acts (NDAAs) to identify continuing, new, and annulled Title 10 (and Title 22) statutes to update the catalog of SC authorities RAND had assembled for the 2013 Security Cooperation Mechanisms report. This provided a baseline of existing authorities current as of the fiscal year (FY) 2016 NDAA. The team then categorized the Title 10 authorities according to the framework set forth in Chapter Three; this categorized list of 2016 authorities is offered in Appendix A. Chapter Four overlays the challenges identified in Chapter Two and the framework onto the catalog of Title 10 authorities to propose "major muscle movements" that would reduce redundancies, fill gaps, and enhance utility of the 2016 authorities. Were the proposed changes enacted, the new, simplified catalog of authorities would appear in the Appendix B list.

Finally, Chapter Five offers some concluding remarks and posits the benefits that could accrue to SC stakeholders were proposed changes to be enacted.

It is important to capture a number of caveats regarding the research behind this report. First, our focus is on Title 10 authorities only; it was outside the scope of this research to suggest changes to Title 22 SC authorities or those in other titles of U.S. Code. The interaction between Title 10 and Title 22 authorities is an important issue that touches on the roles of the Departments of State and Defense in U.S. relationships with other nations. Second, while our discussions did touch on challenges derived from DoD's internal SC processes, addressing these was not part of our task.[5] Finally, the report examines the Title 10 authorities most commonly used by the CCMDs and some DoD agencies; a number of remaining authorities, flagged in Chapter Four, were not closely reviewed and should be further investigated.

---

[5] On the other hand, Moroney, Thaler, and Hogler (2013) explicitly addressed DoD processes.

CHAPTER TWO

DoD Challenges in Utilizing Title 10 Authorities

The U.S. Congress expresses its intent for execution and oversight of SC through legislation that authorizes and constrains interactions with partner nations by the executive branch, including the DoD. Each year, Congress may add, repeal, adjust, or extend authorities based on requests from the DoD or other U.S. government agencies, changes in the security environment, or emerging concerns by individual members of Congress. In a number of cases, authorities continue into subsequent years by default when they are not time-constrained (or when a termination date set by a sunset provision has not yet been reached) and when Congress sees no need for change.

The congressional effort through Title 10 authorizations in the past decade and a half to improve responsiveness to emerging threats and expand the tools that the U.S. government can use to build partner capacity has greatly enhanced the ability of the DoD to engage foreign nations. For example, the Coalition Readiness Support Program (CRSP), authorized through a number of Title 10 statutes and Public Laws, enabled U.S. European Command (EUCOM) to quickly train and equip less capable allies in Europe to join expeditionary operations in Afghanistan under the International Security Assistance Force (ISAF).[1] Likewise, Section 1206 of the FY 2006 NDAA provided the SecDef the authority to rapidly train and equip foreign military partners for CT and stability operations and has been used widely by DoD. Congress has extended this authority year after year and recently

---

[1]   Moroney, Thaler, and Hogler, 2013, pp. 50–51 and pp. 151–152.

broadened and codified the legislation under Title 10, Section 2282 to allow U.S. military engagement with foreign security forces that conduct border security or CT but are in ministries or departments other than the ministry of defense (MoD).[2] DoD has employed these newer authorities along with authorities already on the books to greatly expand opportunities to work with partners and thereby support key U.S. objectives overseas.

However, as indicated in Chapter One, the catalog of 123 Title 10 authorities relating to SC has become rather unwieldy and has helped make delivery of SC increasingly difficult for the DoD personnel who develop, plan, and execute initiatives with foreign partners.[3] This chapter describes the challenges these personnel face in pursuing efforts to educate, train, equip, exercise with, and otherwise support partner nations in achieving common objectives. Our focus is on the authorities themselves and much less so on the processes, resources, and organizational relationships that accompany the authorities, though our recommendations have implications for these other elements of SC.[4]

The RAND study team drew insights from prior research and set out to broaden the understanding of the challenges the SC workforce in the DoD faces in employing Title 10 authorities to plan and execute SC activities. This involved nonattributable, focused discussions with all the CCMDs, some of their component commands, military services, offices in OSD, and defense agencies. Armed with the list of existing SC authorities (described in Chapter Four) and a background understanding of challenges, the team developed protocols of questions designed to elicit insight on:

- authorities the organization deals with on a frequent basis and for what purposes

---

[2]   Some governments use "department of defense" rather than "ministry of defense." We use the term "ministry of defense" (MoD) to capture agencies dedicated to national defense.

[3]   And, as previously indicated, the Title 10 authorities are in addition to statutes in Title 22 and other legislation, as well as programs that arise out of appropriations rather than authorizations.

[4]   Moroney, Thaler, and Hogler (2013) focused on processes, programs, resources, and organizational relationships.

- challenges these organizations face in using the authorities, and where authorities are working well
- ideas for change to mitigate some of these challenges.

The challenges that emerged from these discussions fall into three general areas of concern. First, the proliferation of authorities, their complexity, and unsynchronized requirements make it exceedingly difficult to develop and manage SC initiatives with partners. Second, the lack of predictability in funding available from year to year and the constraints on how and when funds can be used inhibit planning and execution of SC. And third, new threats to U.S. national interests are emerging that existing authorities lack the flexibility to adequately address. We describe these challenges in the following section of this chapter. It should also be noted that many of the discussions touched on problems with myriad processes—often internal to DoD—that have arisen around the development and implementation of SC initiatives and programs. While we do note some of these issues, the authorities themselves are the main focus of our analysis.

In addition, the RAND study team initiated discussions on Title 10 SC authorities with House and Senate staffers on Capitol Hill from both parties who work on SC-related legislative initiatives. Initially, our discussions were with individuals or small groups of staffers about their insights on SC authorities. Subsequently, we led a workshop on the Hill that included staffers from multiple committees and offices of members of Congress, as well as officials from OSD, the Joint Staff, and the Department of State (DoS). We first provided the entire list of Title 10 authorities and presented the challenges we heard from interlocutors in DoD and asked staffers to provide their perspectives on these challenges. Then, we engaged the staffers in a discussion of alternative approaches to simplifying Title 10 authorities, including through consolidation and revision. We summarize these discussions and offer concluding remarks later in this chapter.

DoD Components See Title 10 Security Cooperation Authorities as Both Enabling and Confounding

In RAND discussions with multiple stakeholders in DoD over the past several years, it has been rare to hear that commanders and other decisionmakers were unable to achieve their SC objectives because authorities were not available to do so.[5] Generally, we heard that "there is always a way to reach the end-state that you want, but maybe not as fast or as easily as you would want,"[6] and that the need to work through the complexities of the authorities to employ them was often "painful."[7] Moreover, there were signs that the inefficiencies associated with Title 10 authorities tend to waste resources. One discussant likened the authorities maze to the tax code in that existing authorities are maintained as new authorities are added.[8] Another noted that "we really just need more flexibility in what we already have available to us."[9] At the same time, however, stakeholders contended that any efforts at reforming Title 10 authorities should "do no harm" to those that have worked well. Moreover, while an array of small, disjointed funding streams may be very challenging to synchronize, they are also much less of a target for large-scale budget cuts than large funding pools. The following sections summarize the challenges that DoD SC personnel face in using the Title 10 authorities to deliver SC to partner nations around the world.

Enactment of new authorities to fill gaps and broaden DoD's capacity to work with partners has resulted in increasing complexity and the emergence of what SC stakeholders refer to as a "patchwork" of authorities and associated tools (programs, resources, etc.) that they must carefully weave together to build partner capacity and conduct

---

[5]   There was a small set of exceptions to this, as detailed later in this chapter.

[6]   Discussion with DoD officials, April 23, 2015.

[7]   A descriptor used by multiple interlocutors across DoD during discussions with RAND from 2012–2015. See also Moroney, Thaler, and Hogler, 2013, pp. 29–58.

[8]   Discussion with DoD officials, May 12, 2015.

[9]   Discussion with DoD officials, October 5, 2015.

other SC activities. In prior RAND work, this patchwork was introduced as follows:

> Whereas some might see a patchwork as a work of art that everyone is fond of, is carefully constructed, and lacks holes, the term in our context has negative connotations. This patchwork is more like a tangled web, with holes, overlaps, and confusions. Often, several funding sources are used to support single events, and several programs are used to support broader initiatives. The challenges to planning, resourcing, executing, and assessing BPC activities are considerable. First, authorities for BPC vary considerably. Some authorities attached to programs are single-year, and some are multiyear. Some limit DoD to engaging only with a partner country's military forces, while others allow DoD to engage other armed forces under the authority of ministries other than the Ministry of Defense (MoD). Some allow for training; others do not.[10]

The following sections provide more-detailed insight into the challenges that this patchwork of authorities presents to SC planners, resource managers, and implementers in DoD.

The Negative Effects of Complexity and Proliferation of Authorities

The proliferation of authorities in the past ten to 15 years, many of which have overlapping mandates, has created multiple challenges for SC stakeholders in DoD who work hard to deliver SC within the bounds of the law. These authorities detail different requirements and constraints that determine with whom DoD can work, on what, under what circumstances, and how and when DoD must notify or report to Congress on particular initiatives. This has introduced a great deal of complexity into the system and requires SC personnel to exhibit an understanding of the available statutes that many liken to that of an experienced lawyer. Consider, however, that the active-duty military members who comprise a large portion of the SC workforce often enter their assignments in combatant and component commands with little

---

[10] Moroney, Thaler, and Hogler, 2013, p. xv.

experience in SC and rotate out every two to three years, taking with them whatever knowledge and experience they gained. DoD civilians who remain longer in their positions are therefore crucial resources in the DoD SC enterprise, but they are fewer in number. However, even with their considerable experience, they find it difficult to use a number of Title 10 authorities. To complicate matters, Congress establishes a new NDAA each year that at times uses different reference (or section) numbers for previously legislated authorities that have been revised, and SC personnel in the field must track these changes and refer to them when requesting funds.[11]

One of the most oft-heard challenges relates to the need to apply multiple Title 10 authorities (sometimes in combination with Title 22 authorities) to legally implement a single event or initiative with a foreign country. As one discussant related, "cobbling together several authorities to make [a single event] happen is time-consuming and painful—and it requires someone with intimate knowledge of the arcane authorities process," something rotating military members rarely possess.[12] Another lamented the "cocktail" of 12 authorities needed to fund exercises, and that it is a "full-time gig" to figure out how to legally apply the different pots of money.[13] Authorities that must be used together have different funding streams or sources, cycles, processes, restrictions, and congressional notification and reporting requirements.[14]

This need to combine authorities is the most-visible manifestation of the patchwork among DoD SC stakeholders, and discussants provided multiple instances of it. For example, the Georgia Deployment Program, a two-year train-and-equip initiative from 2009 to 2011 to help four Georgian infantry battalions deploy on six-month rotations to Afghanistan with the U.S. Marines under ISAF, required five separate authorities:

[11] Discussion with DoD officials, April 24, 2015.

[12] Discussion with DoD officials, May 8, 2015.

[13] Discussion with DoD officials, May 5, 2015.

[14] Discussions with DoD officials, April 16, 2015, and May 12, 2015.

- previously allocated Title 22, Foreign Military Financing (FMF), to fund the program start in FY09
- CRSP for training and loaned training equipment in FY10
- Section 1202, an Enhanced Acquisition and Cross Servicing Agreement, for deployment equipment and vehicles in FY10 and FY11
- Section 2010, Developing Countries Combined Exchange Program (DCCEP), for a mission rehearsal exercise in FY10
- Section 1206 for equipment permanently supplied to Georgia in FY10.[15]

Similarly, a loan of Mine Resistant Ambush Protected (MRAP) vehicles to another country for participation in ISAF required six authorities for equipment, training, and sustainment, including CRSP, Foreign Military Sales (FMS), Section 1206, and Section 1202.[16] But when the funding for one authority falls through, "everything falls apart" like a "house of cards" whereby an "entire program may collapse."[17] When one must combine multiple events and initiatives to pursue a comprehensive SC program in a partner nation, the complexity becomes onerous.

The proliferation of Title 10 authorities that are highly specific with regard to geographic, mission, activity, partner, and timing restrictions has created what many SC personnel perceive as severe inefficiencies and renders application of multiple authorities for single events highly problematic. Such inefficiencies require staff to focus on navigating bureaucracy rather than strategic planning. In the case of military-to-military (mil-mil) authorities, for instance, geographic restrictions have left some CCMDs without easily attainable means of covering the personnel expenses of less-developed countries that are participating in conferences, seminars, and other such events. Similar but theater-targeted authorities exist for the U.S. Southern Command

---

[15] Michael Stuber, "Special Funding and Authorities Available to the Combatant Command," EUCOM briefing at ECCM Conference, May 3, 2011, slide 35.

[16] Discussion with DoD officials, April 24, 2015.

[17] Discussion with DoD officials, October 5, 2015; Stuber, 2011, slide 36.

(SOUTHCOM; Section 1050, Latin American Cooperation) and the U.S. Africa Command (AFRICOM; Section 1050A, African Cooperation), while the U.S. Pacific Command (PACOM) uses a program called the Asia-Pacific Regional Initiative (APRI). U.S. Central Command (CENTCOM) and EUCOM must use Traditional Commander's Activity (TCA) funds or the global Section 1051 "Multilateral, bilateral, or regional cooperation programs," which requires permission from OSD for every event (and there are hundreds of events per year in each CCMD) and must compete with other authorities in terms of funding.[18] For these other CCMDs there is "no deep pot for personnel expenses," requiring them to pursue alternative funding sources and compete with other programs for scarce funding. A number of discussants suggested that it would be better not to have geographical restrictions on such authorities to simplify them and to facilitate planning and coordination across CCMDs, whose interests often align even when the seams or lines between the commands do not.[19]

Likewise, some authorities restrict the types of partner nations or organizations with which DoD can work. Eligibility of a partner nation for DCCEP funding (to defray expenses for participation in a joint exercise with U.S. forces) is based on whether the partner meets economic and governmental thresholds of developing countries from the World Bank and other international organizations. One participating partner may cross this threshold in the planning phase of an event and suddenly is no longer eligible—and there is no transition time—while another participant remains eligible. Partners express their concern about the United States lowering costs for some partners and not for others, and may interpret this in terms of relative "value" of a partner to the United States, causing problems or inconsistencies in the U.S.-partner relationships.[20]

---

[18] Discussions with DoD officials, May 7–8, 2015.

[19] Discussions with DoD officials, April 24, 2015, and May 7–8, 2015.

[20] Discussions with DoD officials, April 29, 2015, May 5, 2015, and May 7–8, 2015. SC planners may request waivers for individual events for countries that have lost eligibility, but this is seen as a complication that requires more man-hours.

For a number of authorities, DoD is limited to working only with foreign military forces that are under partner MoDs. However, when it comes to CT, security forces under non-MoD entities such as ministries or departments of interior may conduct the bulk of the planning and operations, or may conduct CT operations in concert with their MoDs. Inability to conduct mil-mil and training events with these non-MoD security forces limits DoD's ability to achieve key objectives.[21] This has caused CCMDs to use "indirect" means to achieve some objectives—e.g., supporting the use by other U.S. government agencies of counternarcotics (CN) authorities to train partner security forces in skills in common with CT skills, or using CT funds to build a perimeter fence because CT military instruction will be conducted at the site.[22] In other cases, authorities are "stretched," as in the case of Section 2011 Joint Combined Exchange Training (JCET) for special operations forces (SOF), in which exercises with partner SOF are supposed to focus on training of U.S. forces but sometimes involve enhancing capabilities of the partner.[23]

Similarly, authorities that restrict activities to specific mission areas are seen as inflexible in the face of quickly emerging threats, making it difficult to build partner capacity in intended mission areas and further impelling SC personnel to "game" the system to achieve their SC objectives. After 2001 and until recently, the priority for U.S. national security strategy and for SC (and DoD activity in particular) has been counterterrorism.[24] Congress established Section 1206 and many other recent SC authorities on the basis of the need to rapidly respond (and help partners respond) to threats from al-Qaeda and more

---

[21] Discussions with DoD officials, April 24, 2015, and October 14, 2015. U.S. Code, Title 10, Section 2282, Authority to Build the Capacity of Foreign Security Forces (October 15, 2015), now includes language that allows DoD to work on CT with "national-level security forces," which could include non-MoD forces.

[22] Discussion with DoD officials, May 6, 2015.

[23] Discussion with DoD officials, April 23, 2015; Moroney, Thaler, and Hogler, 2013, p. 41.

[24] For example, "Counter Terrorism and Irregular Warfare" was the first mission listed under "Primary Missions of the U.S. Armed Forces" in the 2012 Defense Strategic Guidance. See U.S. Department of Defense, *Sustaining U.S. Global Leadership: Priorities for 21st Century Defense*, January 2012, p. 4.

recently the Islamic State of Iraq and the Levant (ISIL). But as the CT mission area has been addressed in the past ten to 15 years, other missions have emerged that are becoming priorities for the United States and its partners but that are not explicitly covered under the CT rubric (or under "stability operations," another area addressed in authorities). These other emerging areas include cyber warfare and "hybrid" warfare of the type Russia has utilized to subjugate eastern Ukraine and annex Crimea (gaps are also addressed in a subsequent section of this chapter). Capstone DoD strategic planning guidance that defines priorities and directs the efforts of the CCMDs also identifies nontraditional threats, such as transnational border security, maritime security, and foreign fighters.[25] While Congress and the administration have created some specific programs to bolster Ukraine and eastern NATO allies,[26] existing authorities do not provide the flexibility for SC personnel to pursue these mission areas in other nations or regions. Thus, they are left with "stretching" existing authorities to achieve key objectives with partners.[27]

The proliferation of complicated authorities has led to a number of pernicious effects in DoD's SC enterprise. Two deserve mention here. First, authorities and related programs require that staff in DoD stakeholder organizations—particularly the CCMDs, OSD, and the agencies—are available to plan their use and develop initiatives or events, shepherd them through the myriad justification and approval processes, and manage and report on their execution. The greater the number of authorities required to achieve stakeholder objectives, the larger the staff required to properly manage them. But at the same time, the catalog of authorities has expanded, while budget cuts have required staff contraction across DoD. This leaves stakeholders with "too many programs…and not enough people to execute" because "we

---

[25] Discussions with DoD officials, May 7–8, 2015.

[26] These include Public Law 113-272, Ukraine Freedom Support Act of 2014, Section 6, Increased Military Assistance for the Government of Ukraine, December 18, 2014; Public Law 113-291, Carl Levin and Howard P. "Buck" McKeon National Defense Authorization Act for Fiscal Year 2015, Section 1535, European Reassurance Initiative, December 19, 2014.

[27] Discussions with DoD officials, April 24, 2015, May 5, 2015, and May 7–8, 2015.

are losing people who manage the programs."[28] While OSD has at times sought to hone a reach-back capacity to provide advice to the CCMDs, the expanding catalog of authorities still requires a larger staff to properly manage them. This forces SC personnel to consider the cost-benefit of doing some events with multiple funding sources given the man-hours and workload required to manage use of separate authorities, whereby "small programs aren't worth the time."[29] This also leads to programs that are not executable in the field.[30]

Second, a natural outcome of this complex patchwork is the increasing role of legal interpretation of the authorities by DoD counsel to ensure that initiatives with foreign nations are pursued within the bounds of the law and congressional intent. These interpretations can change, sometimes quickly and based on the particular legal counsel making the determination.[31] This is not a criticism of DoD legal counsel, but rather a call for greater clarity and simplicity in the authorities themselves to minimize the potential for alternative interpretations of the law (some of which change from year to year) when it comes to SC activities. One important example of reinterpretation of authorities affecting SC efforts relates to the use of Section 168 (Military-to-Military Contacts and Comparable Activities) to fund mil-mil engagements and events. Prior to 2012, SC personnel in the CCMDs had used this flexible statute to apply TCA operations and maintenance (O&M) funds to mil-mil events; EUCOM was using it to support 700 events a year. In mid-2012, OSD's Office of the General Counsel interpreted the statute as requiring a yearly appropriation that is not delegated to the CCMDs, but to the SecDef. EUCOM and other CCMDs stopped using the authority and had to cancel events or quickly revise mil-mil

---

[28] Discussions with DoD officials, April 24, 2015, May 5, 2015, and May 7–8, 2015.

[29] Discussion with DoD officials, May 7, 2015.

[30] For example, Special Operations Command-Africa was unable to execute $3–4 million in Global Security Contingency Fund money against Boko Haram because it did not have the manpower for administrative duties related to the program, such as cutting travel orders. Discussion with DoD officials, May 6, 2015.

[31] Discussions with DoD officials, May 5, 2015, May 7–8, 2015, April 29, 2015, and October 14, 2015.

event funding plans in mid-stream.[32] It has also led to a reduction in highly valued National Guard Bilateral Affairs Officers in EUCOM, whose allowances were paid through Section 168. This has led some to ask, "Is 168 a valid authority?"[33] Thus, lack of clarity in congressional intent in authority language has created uncertainty as to how authorities can be legally used. Inconsistent legal interpretations of authorities from year to year can make it difficult for SC personnel to plan both internally and with foreign partners in some cases because of uncertainty as to whether activities can be pursued.

Unpredictability in Funding Inhibits Planning and Execution

A second general area of concern for DoD's SC workforce relates to the unpredictability in Title 10 SC funding to enable planning of initiatives and activities and the constraints on application of funds in execution. Many DoD discussants indicated that the DoD strategic planning guidance mandates a five-year planning horizon, yet Title 10 funding is available in much-shorter–term one- or two-year increments. This injects an enormous amount of "guess-work"—according to one discussant, "We are always gaming, guessing how much we think we are going to get"[34]—into planning and limits predictability and flexibility.[35] According to another, "the Department lacks the ability to engage in long-term activities with partner nations.… Programs are episodic, and are generally not sustainable."[36] This has had deleterious effects in a number of ways.

First, the Theater Campaign Plans (TCPs) that guide SC, operations, posture, and other activities within a CCMD often are approved despite lack of insight into whether the programs to achieve TCP objec-

---

[32] Discussions with DoD officials, May 7–8, 2015. See also Contract and Fiscal Law Department, *Fiscal Law Desk Book 2014, Chapter 10: Operational Funding,* Charlottesville, Va.: The Judge Advocate General's School, U.S. Department of Defense, December 2014; and Moroney, Thaler, and Hogler, 2013, p. 53.

[33] Discussions with DoD officials, May 7–8, 2015.

[34] Discussion with DoD officials, May 6, 2015.

[35] Discussions with DoD officials, April 16, 2015, and May 6, 2015.

[36] Discussion with DoD officials, May 8, 2015.

tives will be available.[37] Strategic guidance mandates that DoD components develop five-year plans and identify how they intend to achieve their theater objectives in that time. But these DoD components do not know how much funding they will receive for SC under Title 10 beyond one or two years and can only speculate on what is possible in the third, fourth, and fifth years. For example, Section 1203, a relatively new authority that allows U.S. general purpose forces (GPF) to train with partner GPF (in a manner akin to the well-regarded JCET program for SOF), is intended to enable training of U.S. forces while furthering partnerships with foreign military forces. Yet it does not come with funding, and must compete for O&M funds that are sorely needed elsewhere, including for operational readiness of U.S. forces.[38] Representatives from a number of CCMDs have said they do not use Section 1203 or, if they do, only rarely. With no funding, it is difficult to assume it can be used in planning one year, much less five years, hence.

Second, the partner nations that stand to benefit from SC programs are unable to plan or budget their own efforts, particularly if they are planning to receive equipment from the United States and will need to program their own funds for sustainment and maintenance of that equipment. This is a critical aspect of SC: The partner nation should have "skin in the game" to ensure the viability of an SC initiative over the longer term. The unpredictability that one- or two-year money engenders can also sour partners on U.S. cooperative efforts and make it difficult for partners to develop sustainment plans. In one recent case, funding for major end items for the Czech Republic had to be cut mid-stream because the length of time required to procure the items did not align with the more limited time during which funds would be available. The sudden instability and delay in an important initiative was an embarrassment and required SC planners to quickly find alternative sources of funding.[39]

---

[37] Discussion with DoD officials, May 7, 2015.

[38] Discussions with DoD officials, May 5, 2015, and October 5, 2015.

[39] Discussions with DoD officials, May 7–8, 2015.

This raises a third issue—that of viability of even a short-term program under the funding timelines in many Title 10 authorities. For example, prior to a Section 2282 unit train-and-equip or Section 1033 counternarcoterrorism initiative, funds must be obligated before the end of the FY in which they are approved. When approval comes late in the year, those SC personnel requesting the funds may only have a month or two to properly budget and award contracts associated with the initiative or risk losing the funding.[40] For some types of complex equipment, such as Intelligence, Surveillance, and Reconnaissance pods for aircraft, it is not always possible to get the equipment on contract in time.[41] This is not an efficient way to contract complex work or to plan training regimens and reserve trainers for particular time slots, and SC personnel report that they need more lead-time. Mil-mil events, such as conferences, seminars, and exchanges, are executed with one-year money. In many cases, particularly with less-developed partner nations, conditions are quite fluid, and some countries just do not show up as planned. But the authorities do not allow for flexibility to respond to these conditions, and sometimes CCMDs receive funds in December, leaving only nine months to execute.[42] Single-year funding streams do not provide the continuity desired in working with partners because follow-on funding cannot be guaranteed.[43] Likewise, some military construction funding—such as that proposed for the South China Sea initiative to enhance regional maritime security— is only available for one year and is a challenge to execute for such complex projects.[44] Some interlocutors suggest that two-year money would allow greater flexibility in spending authority for mil-mil events

---

[40] This is of course tied to the length of time some of the internal DoD justification and approval processes require to procure the funding in the first place. Section 2282 approvals (like Section 1206 that it replaced) are considered and given in "tranches" throughout the fiscal year; those initiatives considered later in the year are under the greatest time pressure to obligate approved funds before the end of the fiscal year.

[41] Discussion with DoD officials, May 5, 2015.

[42] Discussion with DoD officials, May 5, 2015.

[43] Discussion with DoD officials, May 15, 2015.

[44] Discussion with DoD officials, October 14, 2015.

and other activities.[45] It would also allow for return of unused money and appropriate repurposing of that money when conditions on the ground change—for example, under Section 2010 DCCEP, which is reimbursable and thus awaits the arrival of final receipts from partners who are not limited to the U.S. FY structure.[46]

On the back end of Title 10 train-and-equip initiatives, such as Section 2282, problems arise when equipment arrival is delayed and training (on both operational use and maintenance) cannot be accomplished within the timeframe of the initiative. At that point, SC personnel may scramble to develop a new case or find other funding sources to keep the initiative going. One discussant noted as an example that unmanned aerial vehicles on contract in September may not deliver until April, and then not get shipped to the partner nation until July. By this time, the end of the FY is only a few months away, although it is expected that the partner will be fully trained to use the equipment. However, the funding stream expires by then. Acquisition of equipment is complex, coming from different DoD organizations, and the full equipment package often does not arrive before training must commence.[47] For training to be available, the SC manager would need to send a notification to Congress for an additional year of funding, possibly under a new, different program just to sustain the previous one.[48] For such train-and-equip authorities as Section 2282, discussants suggest that money available for three years after it is obligated (with full operational capability by the end of the third year) would allow SC personnel to advise and assess partner nation progress and then adjust the program if conditions change.[49] Congress has provided

---

[45] Discussion with DoD officials, May 5, 2015.

[46] Discussion with DoD officials, October 14, 2015.

[47] Discussion with DoD officials, October 5, 2015.

[48] Discussion with DoD officials, May 21, 2015.

[49] Discussions with DoD officials, May 5, 2015, and May 6, 2015.

an optional third year to Section 2282 initiatives in response to these difficulties, but it is too early to tell how well this will work.[50]

While restrictions on timing and funding in Title 10 authorities have been a source of frustration among many SC personnel, most understand that such limitations are extremely important to Congress, which relies on them to ensure its oversight of DoD engagements with foreign nations. Yearly justifications to Congress of intended expenditure of funds under specific authorities allow legislators to ensure that DoD is continuing programs and changes to those programs within the outlines of congressional intent. But one might consider the idea that justifications and availability of funding need not be linked, whereby Congress could receive yearly justifications for two-year funding streams in a way that continues to support its oversight function. Conversely, some SC stakeholders in DoD see great value in one- or two-year money because of the "urgency" it represents. One suggested that it "keeps everyone focused on getting something done" and that "we have moved a lot of things this way."[51] Thus, there is a realization in DoD that multiyear (also known as "x-year") funds are not necessarily a panacea to problems with SC authorities, but that some relaxation of limitations might be warranted in certain cases.

Authorities Lack Flexibility to Address Emerging Threats and Other Requirements

We refer to lack of flexibility in authorities in a previous section; this has led to "gaming" behavior—even embarrassment in relationships— as SC personnel need to stretch the intent of the authorities to fill per-

---

[50] Under paragraph (c)(4)(C) of Section 2282, Achievement of Full Operational Capability:

> "If, in accordance with subparagraph (A), equipment is delivered under a program under the authority in subsection (a) in the fiscal year after the fiscal year in which the program begins, amounts for supplies, training, defense services, and small-scale military construction associated with such equipment and necessary to ensure that the recipient unit achieves full operational capability for such equipment may be used in the fiscal year in which the foreign country takes receipt of such equipment and in the next fiscal year." See U.S. Code, Title 10, Section 2282, 2015.

[51] Discussion with DoD officials, April 24, 2015.

ceived gaps in their ability to achieve SC objectives. In one case, discussants spoke of two seminars held recently in Poland and Estonia to share ideas and best practices and gain "intellectual interoperability" with allies with regard to Russian activities. These seminars took months of preparation and required considerable funding by the host nations, but at the last minute there was a cost increase because U.S. statute did not allow DoD to fund the coffee because the forums were not CT-related.[52] Emerging threats (e.g., to cyber operations or maritime security) create some of these gaps, but there are also gaps that emerge from other needs, such as the need to sustain equipment that has been provided to partners through Title 10 authorities.

In the case of cybersecurity, some CCMDs are getting requests from partners to help them improve their capabilities but note that they "can't do it."[53] While the belief may not yet be widespread that a relative lack of authorities for cyber security is a problem, there is growing recognition of the importance of this domain and that partners' weakness in cyber security is also U.S. weakness given that U.S. strategy depends on the support and competence of those partners. Some DoD stakeholders with whom we engaged indicated that they found no reasonable authority for building cyber capacity and thus could not conduct exchanges or training with a range of partners in this area, especially in the case of countries that cannot afford to send their personnel to relevant schools.[54] There have been attempts to apply Section 1206 to cyber BPC activities, but this is one of those "gaming" situations mentioned above and is suboptimal. Stakeholders note that cyber should be more integrated into engagements with partners, and that they would like broader authority to work with them. They point out that the SC community can be slow to respond to a dynamic and changing security environment, and that greater focus on building cyber capacity is warranted. This appears to be a critical need, as U.S.

---

[52] Discussion with DoD officials, May 7, 2015.

[53] Discussion with DoD officials, April 24, 2015.

[54] Discussion with DoD officials, May 5, 2015.

forces overseas "rely on our partners for critical infrastructure [in their countries]: energy, power, telecommunications, and water."[55]

Maritime security is a second area mentioned as an emerging area of non-CT engagement with partners but lacking appropriate global authorities.[56] PACOM officials had sought to obtain funding to improve the capacity of countries facing CN and other maritime threats along the South China Sea and only recently obtained specific authority limited to that subregion under the FY 2016 NDAA to provide maritime assistance and training. EUCOM officials have particular concerns over maritime border security from refugee flows, smuggling, and inter-state competition. They lament the difficulty in helping Southern European states improve their capacity to monitor and respond to refugees pouring in from the Middle East and North Africa.[57] CENTCOM officials seek authority for maritime security, which is not considered CT, because of the expansion of ISIL operations beyond Iraq and Syria. CCMDs find CN authorities (like Section 1004, Support for Counter-Drug Activities) as the most flexible means (the easiest to stretch) to obtain the resources needed to run operations because they can create "a nexus in the explanation for the application of funds" between CN and other mission areas.[58]

SC personnel at EUCOM, U.S. Army Europe, CENTCOM, and PACOM have indicated that they are limited in their abilities to engage in information sharing with foreign forces on issues of ballistic missile defense (BMD) and to provide BMD training, a third mission gap of concern. Mil-mil engagement, exercises, and train-and-equip authorities are not expansive enough to cover BMD and only permit

---

[55] Discussion with DoD officials, April 24, 2015.

[56] Discussion with DoD officials, April 24, 2015. DoD has conducted CT-related maritime engagements with partners under Section 1206.

[57] Discussions with DoD officials, May 7–8, 2015.

[58] Discussions with DoD officials, May 5, 2015, and May 12, 2015. Section 1263, South China Sea Initiative, of the FY 2016 NDAA authorizes the SecDef to provide training assistance to national military or other security forces for the purpose of increasing maritime security and maritime domain awareness of foreign countries along the South China Sea. But this is not global.

some training on unclassified systems. Congress has also expressed its concern over the ballistic missile threat from North Korea and Iran and the need for the United States to cooperate with regional allies on BMD issues to counter those threats in a sense of Congress in Public Law 112-239, and in Section 229 and Public Law 113-66 and Public Law 113-291.[59]

In terms of other mission areas and activities, DoD stakeholders also have indicated that they lack the flexibility in authorities to conduct intelligence sharing and training, defense institution building (DIB), "preventive" BPC for CT, the aforementioned hybrid warfare, and sustainment of U.S.-provided partner equipment. Inability to promote a flow of critical information across regions (especially with regard to transnational threats) and across security organizations (including law enforcement)—and to ensure interoperability through training—is seen as a gap that hamstrings the development of appropriate responses to changing threats.[60] DIB programs have been difficult to execute, are "drops in the bucket" in relation to what is needed at all (not just top) levels of partner security institutions, and are long-term investments requiring strategic patience that are handcuffed by one-year authorities.[61] And lack of authorities for BPC to prevent the rise of terrorist groups is an issue championed especially in the SOUTHCOM area of responsibility (AOR)—where Section 1206 and Section 2282 have not been made available because there is no "active" CT operation—with regard to Lebanese Hezbollah and al-Qaeda.[62]

---

[59] Discussions with DoD officials, May 5, 2015, May 7–8, 2015, April 24, 2015, and October 14, 2015. See also Moroney, Thaler, and Hogler, 2013, pp. 54–57. Public Law 112-239, Section 229, states that it is the sense of the Congress that "the threat from regional ballistic missiles, particularly from Iran and North Korea, is serious and growing, and puts at risk forward-deployed forces, assets, and facilities." Public Law 113-66 and Public Law 113-291 encourage the United States to cooperate with regional allies on BMD issues to enhance the security of all partners.

[60] Discussions with DoD officials, May 5, 2015, and May 7–8, 2015.

[61] Discussions with DoD officials, May 7–8, 2015.

[62] Discussion with DoD officials, April 29, 2015; Moroney, Thaler, and Hogler, 2013, pp. 43–46.

Sustainment—including providing long-term maintenance of U.S.-provided equipment, logistics support, and training partners to maintain a cadre of personnel to employ and sustain the equipment— is one of the most-commonly stated gaps in existing Title 10 authorities. Multiple interlocutors point to the availability of authorities and two-year funding for train-and-equip programs for CT and stability ops, but indicate that equipment often becomes a "static display" for lack of spare parts and maintenance after that short-term money dries up.[63] This is particularly the case among less-developed partners who do not have the wherewithal or the understanding to put in place sustainment programs of their own. There is reluctance on the part of DoS to commit Title 22 FMF funds to support sustainment of the large amounts of equipment provided under Section 1206 and other Title 10 programs. FMF funds are very limited for all but a few select countries, and sustainment of Title 10 initiatives is not an intended role for FMF (although there have been some exceptions). But stakeholders also point out that it does not make sense to sustain a capability into the future in some cases. For example, if the United States provides trucks that a CT partner has run for 200,000 miles and they have achieved objectives set for them, sustainment of those trucks may not be warranted.[64] They indicate that planning for train-and-equip initiatives should include an analysis of the costs and benefits of sustaining the targeted capability beyond the end-date, and some realistic assessment of the sources of sustainment if the analysis suggests it would benefit U.S. (and partner) interests.[65] But the fact remains that Title 10 authority to sustain is extremely limited.

Three other limitations or gaps have been raised in numerous discussions with SC personnel in DoD. We indicated above that DoD has been limited in some authorities to working only with foreign forces associated with national defense agencies. Emerging transnational threats and mission areas require the ability to work with interior agency forces or other gendarme or civil authorities when their security

---

[63] Discussion with DoD officials, May 12, 2015.

[64] Discussion with DoD officials, May 6, 2015.

[65] Discussions with DoD officials, May 5, 2015, and May 6, 2015.

forces retain primary responsibility for those mission areas or operate in close collaboration with MoDs. For example, in many cases, the ministry or department of interior is responsible for securing national infrastructure and cyber assets; of six countries CENTCOM officials are engaging on infrastructure security, only in Jordan is the military responsible for protecting the country's infrastructure.[66]

A second gap in Title 10 authorities is in the flexibility for DoD to work with regional organizations rather than just bilaterally with national governments. Under Title 10, even regional programs (such as the Counterterrorism Partnership Fund [CTPF]) are implemented bilaterally with national governments. There are no mechanisms for training and equipping regional organizations.[67] When this limitation is combined with the limitation on U.S. military engagement with non-MoD security forces, it inhibits the U.S. ability to facilitate coordination among agencies with similar responsibilities within and across partners to have regional effects and to address local security threats.[68]

Finally, while Section 1206 and the subsequent Section 2282 were designed to be a more rapid means of building partner capacity than traditional Title 22 authorities like FMF and FMS, even these programs take some 12-18 months to deliver equipment to partners. A number of SC stakeholders in DoD still perceive a need for more "timely assistance" to partners who require small amounts of support to recover or enhance existing capability of their "forces in the fight."[69] Currently, these stakeholders point out, a "pseudo-FMS" case for $10,000 in truck springs takes the same amount of time to process as a major item of equipment.[70]

---

[66] Discussion with DoD officials, April 24, 2015.

[67] Discussions with DoD officials, May 5, 2015, and May 6, 2015.

[68] Discussion with DoD officials, April 24, 2015.

[69] Discussions with DoD officials, May 6, 2015, and October 14, 2015.

[70] Discussions with DoD officials, May 6, 2015, and April 24, 2015; Moroney, Thaler, and Hogler, 2013, p. 41. One potential vehicle for such procurement is the Special Defense Acquisition Fund, a Title 22 fund that allows provision of defense articles and services in anticipation of their sale or transfer to foreign governments.

Summary of DoD Perceptions of Title 10 SC Authorities

In sum, DoD has been able to achieve many of its SC objectives with the patchwork of Title 10 authorities, but the proliferation of authorities and the complexities they engender have rendered them exceedingly difficult to apply. As we have noted here and in previous research, authorities are not the only reason for the frustration expressed by SC personnel; internal processes, organizational relationships, programmatic requirements, and inadequate levels of funding have also created obstacles. But the existing catalog of Title 10 authorities in some ways drives or complicates these other factors when they present the challenges in planning and execution detailed above. What many in the DoD SC community perceive as a flawed legislative foundation has had a compounding impact on the administration and management of SC programs, systems, and processes.

However, multiple discussants agreed that Title 10 authorities have enabled broader engagement with partners during a period of a rapidly evolving security environment. While recognizing the challenges these authorities present, they also cautioned that any revisions in existing authorities or in how they are structured "do no harm." For example, many pointed to CN authorities as providing unparalleled flexibility to engage, train, and equip partner-nation MoD and non-MoD security forces in this mission area.[71] Authorities for humanitarian assistance and disaster relief are seen as powerful tools that enable training of U.S. and partner civil and military forces while assisting local populations in need.[72] The Section 2249c Regional Defense CTFP has been touted as highly successful in educating future leaders from partner nations on common principles for countering extremist groups.[73] Section 2011 JCETs are seen as a "great tool" for training U.S. SOF and assessing and improving interoperability with partner SOF.[74] Thus, in

---

[71] Discussions with DoD officials, April 24, 2015, April 29, 2015, and October 14, 2015, .

[72] Discussions with DoD officials, April 29, 2015, and October 14, 2015.

[73] Discussion with DoD officials, October 5, 2015.

[74] Discussion with DoD officials, April 23, 2015.

considering consolidation or revision of Title 10 authorities, what is left alone is equally as important as what is changed.

Congressional Concerns Accompany Acknowledgment of Challenges

What are congressional perspectives on the challenges DoD stakeholders say they face, and what might be the way forward? We sought to bring these perspectives to light through a workshop and a series of individual and small-group discussions with congressional staffers to inform both our suggestions for change in Title 10 authorities and OSD's own efforts to pursue reforms. The two-hour workshop included House and Senate staff members from armed services, foreign relations, and appropriations committees and offices of members of Congress, as well as representatives from OSD, the Joint Staff, and DoS.

Congressional staff members we engaged who work with Title 10 SC authorities acknowledge the complexities and challenges the statutes pose to effective SC. They agree with DoD that the manner in which authorities are cobbled together in a patchwork, and the affiliated congressional notifications processes, create problems both for DoD and Congress. They point out that both DoD and Congress are responsible for the "hackneyed genesis" of the existing Title 10 authorities structure—DoD because it asks frequently for new authorities in an *ad hoc* manner and Congress for allowing this "tactical" approach and adding its own requirements (such as multiple reports to many committees) without demanding a strategic rationalization of the authorities.[75] While the staffers recognize the cumbersome nature of the patchwork, however, there is some reluctance to make major changes to Title 10. As one staffer noted in relation to yearly OSD and CCMD requests for new authorities, "everyone hates the patchwork until they don't have the patchwork, but it works the way it is."[76] But they do see room for improvement and simplification.

---

[75] Discussion with congressional staff members, Washington, D.C., May 22, 2015.

[76] Discussion with congressional staff members, Washington, D.C., June 5, 2015.

Some congressional staffers with whom we spoke indicated that Congress may be willing to consider modifications to Title 10 SC authorities through consolidation and revision that broaden and or clarify activities the DoD can pursue to build partnerships and partner capacity. But embedded in this willingness is caution as to the amount of flexibility Congress can offer to DoD and the oversight that modified authorities would provide. According to these staffers, Congress is not willing to cede discretionary spending to DoD in a way that encroaches on the foreign policy role of DoS or on its own oversight responsibilities.

For example, staffers suggested that there are limits to which Congress will allow comprehensive "umbrella" authorities that DoD might seek for simplification and reduction in numbers of statutes. At its inception, Section 1207 Global Security Contingency Fund (GSCF) was a pilot program to be used for unforeseen contingencies that could not be addressed in normal systems and processes. It was to be used by exception rather than as a primary tool. But it came to be seen as a "be-all end-all" umbrella authority that would provide multiyear funds to train-and-equip partner MoD and non-MoD security forces in a range of mission areas, and thereby help address preferences of the CCMDs.[77] The concept was to provide flexibility to use DoD funds while giving DoS a lead role in the decisionmaking about where to spend them. It took three years and a great deal of congressional work and "horse-trading" to pass the legislation. But GSCF is perceived to have failed because of unwieldy justification and reporting requirements to eight separate congressional committees, the aforementioned internal DoD (and DoS) bureaucratic processes, and obstacles to DoD-DoS inter-agency coordination derived from competition over SC roles. On the last issue, staffers noted that Congress "cannot legislate that DoD and DoS get along."

There is a perception among some congressional staff members that large umbrella authorities have a high potential for misuse, do not achieve stated goals of interagency SC alignment, and simply create added bureaucratic work in DoD and in congressional staffs.

---

[77] RAND workshop, Washington, D.C., July 17, 2015.

Authorities that become too "generic" suffer negative connotations on Capitol Hill. They point out that this is why one of the broadest SC authorities, Title 22 FMF, is frequently "tied up in knots" in committee for many recipient countries.[78] Staffers expressed some preference for smaller targeted "niche" authorities because committee oversight and management are much easier—and in some cases, legislators have equities invested in authorities they originated for issues they believe are of high priority—but understand that in many cases something in between broad "umbrella" and narrow "niche" would be a reasonable way to rationalize the patchwork.

We also heard that an important part of congressional reluctance to make wholesale changes to the structure and content of Title 10 SC authorities is broad agreement over DoD's need to revamp its own internal SC processes. One staffer noted that "the patchwork problem is one of the leading complaints being thrown at Congress, but DoD has never looked at itself.... It created the problem by being mired in its own red tape."[79] The staff members contend that DoD's structures and processes for planning, justifying, and approving SC initiatives have created much of the "churn" that SC personnel in the field face and the "gaming" in which they feel they must engage. Some staffers suggested that Congress would insist that internal reforms to remove bureaucratic obstacles and rationalize processes must take place before—or at least concurrently with—any DoD requests to revise Title 10 SC authorities.

Many staff members pointed to a second element of congressional reluctance to change authorities: frustration that DoD funding requests and justifications tend to be "widget-focused" (on equipment details) and provide little insight into the SC strategy for each partner nation or region and the longer-term national and theater objectives funded programs would achieve. According to these staffers, Congress seeks to have outlined more clearly how justifications for equipment are part of a broader plan. One discussant contended that "if there is rigor on the front end [of a DoD funding request to Congress], more

---

[78] Discussion with congressional staff members, Washington, D.C., June 5, 2015.

[79] RAND workshop, Washington, D.C., July 17, 2015.

flexibility would be given [by Congress] on the back end."[80] Staffers indicated that legislators want to see clear definition of BPC goals, a visible strategy for how Title 10 authorities will fulfill them, and measurable, concrete outcomes for authorities implemented. In fact, in Section 1202 of the FY 2016 NDAA, Congress required "the Secretary of Defense, in coordination with the Secretary of State, to develop a strategic framework for Department of Defense security cooperation to guide prioritization of resources and activities."

Thus, many congressional staffers with whom we engaged see the crux of the problem resting in DoD's management and implementation of authorities. We interpret this as a call for DoD to describe in more detail its plan for using SC to advance broader national security goals. In general, what are the priorities in terms of countries to help, and how? What are the broad SC goals for the next few years, and how do they support higher-level goals? The framework we propose in Chapter Three helps categorize SC activities and authorities that would help answer the "how" question, but it only gets at part of the larger question about goals, partners, and resources.

Many congressional staffers with whom we spoke also note the risk in continuing to emphasize the CT mission at the expense of other strategic challenges like Russia and China, and in this there is broad agreement from DoD stakeholders. In some ways, this is perceived as a strategic question of gaining clarity on what is the "war on terror" and DoD's role in it and how its efforts are measured, yet DoD continues to request new CT-related authorities despite this lack of clarity. Congress realizes, according to these staffers, that at times SC activities associated with CT-specific authorities are stretched in ways that exceed the purposes intended by Congress. Staffers suggest that this "CT myopia" is even reflected in DoD bureaucracy, whereby OSD-Policy's Europe office had to compete through OSD's CT office to obtain funding for Ukraine operations, which they state was "ridiculous" for such a high-priority U.S. interest.[81] Thus, there appears to be congressional support

---

[80] Discussion with congressional staff members, Washington, D.C., May 22, 2015.

[81] Discussion with congressional staff members, Washington, D.C., June 5, 2015.

for breaking out of the CT focus to incorporate other strategic challenges in proposed changes to authorities.

In considering the way ahead, staffers suggested that proposals to consolidate begin with "low-hanging fruit," or those authorities that serve similar purposes or have similar language and can easily be consolidated, such as military academies and other education-related efforts.[82] Success in these areas could help drive consolidation of more complex authorities, as long as consolidation does not lead to overuse or abuse of the authorities. Discussants also cited the political risk associated with seeking to quickly repeal existing authorities in which some legislators have a vested interest. This could complicate efforts to rationalize the patchwork. In sum, there appears to be an opportunity to make changes that would alleviate authorities-based challenges while mitigating congressional concerns.

Conclusions

With regard to rationalizing the patchwork of Title 10 SC authorities, DoD and Congress appear to share some common ground between the challenges facing the SC workforce and the potential willingness of legislators (at least in the view of their staff members) to consider changes that simplify while maintaining congressional oversight requirements. A prominent point of contention is DoD's desire to approach Congress on authorities and congressional desire, as expressed by the staffers we engaged, for DoD to first provide a strategic context for its SC activities and review its internal bureaucratic processes. Consolidating authorities could help to reduce the number of programs and personnel managing them. This could also assist the DoD to better standardize processes and timelines. Conversely, the management of SC programs, systems, and processes stems from provisions in the law. A confused and fragmented legal framework for SC results in organizations and processes that reflect that chaos and requires greater numbers

---

[82] RAND workshop, Washington, D.C., July 17, 2015.

of subject-matter experts and technicians to help the system operate effectively.

One of the first steps to making sense of the patchwork of Title 10 authorities is to offer a logical framework in which to categorize them. This framework is intended to facilitate a systematic mitigation of challenges described in this chapter through improvements in the existing catalog of Title 10 authorities. Subsequently, the framework also should help DoD and Congress work together in formulating and recasting Title 10 SC authorities and provide SC personnel in the field with a more straightforward means of identifying and requesting use of authorities for activities they seek to pursue in building partner capacity and solidifying partnerships. It is such a framework to which we now turn.

CHAPTER THREE

A Framework for Categorizing SC Authorities

Our proposed framework for categorizing SC authorities builds on our discussions with a range of SC stakeholders. As Chapter Two makes clear, the current patchwork of Title 10 SC authorities poses problems for SC personnel in DoD. Some believe they do not have sufficient authority to pursue necessary SC tasks; a larger group contends it spends an inordinate amount of time and effort cobbling together required authority and associated resources. This dissatisfaction has resulted in a consistent demand for a standardized "toolkit" that SC planners at various levels can access and employ as needed without too much trouble. Nevertheless, some of the non-DoD stakeholders we interviewed, or who participated in the Capitol Hill workshop we organized, expressed concern that DoD could overstep its institutional bounds into the realm of foreign policy or undertake activities not in line with congressional intent unless it was given specialized SC tools with detailed instructions regarding when, where, how and with whom they could and could not be used.

As a consequence, the proposed categorization framework both supports DoD's goal of reforming SC authorities and accounts for divergent SC stakeholder perspectives inside and outside DoD, which will inevitably shape the outcome of this effort. Additionally, it sets the stage for further rationalization of SC authorities via consolidation, clarification, broadening, and creation in Chapter Four.

Before turning to our authorities scheme, however, we first review how others, such as the Defense Security Cooperation Agency (DSCA), OSD, the CCMDs, and previous RAND studies, have classified major elements of SC to incorporate their perspectives and ensure that our categorization aligns with the thinking of major SC stakeholders.

Several Ways of Looking at Authorities

While there are few SC-related categorization schemes that focus specifically on authorities, planners and analysts in DoD's SC community have developed quite a few mechanisms for classifying the basic components of SC. In general, these classification approaches focus on *activities* or programs (SC means), *missions* or lines of effort (LOEs) (SC ways), *objectives* or effects (SC ends), or a combination of these elements. Although existing SC categorization frameworks were developed for a variety of reasons, they provide a useful starting point for thinking about alternatives to classify SC authorities for planning and legislative purposes.

Activity-Based Approach

An activity-based approach to categorization organizes authorities by generic SC activity or program type. Such authorities could be used to achieve multiple SC objectives via various LOEs with a range of partner countries. One source for such a classification scheme is the "Greenbook" published by the Defense Institute of Security Assistance Management (DISAM), the training arm of DSCA. DISAM identifies seven categories of SC programs:

- security assistance administered by DoD
- global train-and-equip
- international armaments cooperation
- humanitarian assistance
- training and education
- combined exercises
- contacts.[1]

---

[1]   Defense Institute of Security Assistance Management (DISAM), *The Management of Security Cooperation (Green Book)*, 34.1 ed., August 2015, p. 7.

In the case of contacts, legislation that permits DoD to pay for its own personnel or foreign defense personnel to engage in a variety of mil-mil activities (e.g., visits, meetings, and exchanges) in different regions of the world would constitute an activity-based authority.

Mission-Based Approach

A mission-based classification approach organizes authorities according to the mission that SC activities are intended to advance. The LOEs contained within the CCMDs' TCPs are probably the most-recognized sources for this type of framing mechanism within DoD. These LOEs comprise the operational areas in which the commands intend to focus their resources over the planning period in order to meet national security objectives. While some CCMD LOEs are country- or activity-focused, the majority of them are mission-based. For example, AFRICOM's 2012 TCP listed the following LOEs, among others:

- counterterrorism
- counternarcotics
- counter-weapons of mass destruction
- border security
- maritime security
- peacekeeping.[2]

Drawing on the AFRICOM example, a mission-based global authority might permit DoD personnel in different theaters to engage in mil-mil contacts and train-and-equip activities focusing on maritime security in order to enhance cooperation in this mission area and help build partners' capabilities to manage and protect their territorial waters.

Objective-Based Approach

Another categorization alternative is to organize authorities according to the objectives that SC activities are designed to achieve. Although rarely used as the sole basis for SC classification, objectives are a promi-

---

[2]   DoD, *Security Cooperation Toolkit*, DISAM, accessed June 21, 2012.

nent organizing device in high-level DoD planning and guidance documents. For example, objective-based "focus areas" in DoD guidance of importance to SC planners are: building the capacity and capability of partners, securing operational access for U.S. forces, and establishing positive relationships with U.S. partners.[3]

While such broad objectives can at best serve as top-level classification criteria, it is possible to envision a specific objective-based authority, such as one that enabled DoD to engage in technical exchanges, security assistance, and joint exercises to improve strategic airlift interoperability with multiple partners.

Combinatory Approach

As indicated above, authorities could be organized by more than one SC dimension: e.g., by activity and mission, activity and objective, mission and objective, or activity, mission, and objective. Relational SC databases, such as those maintained by OSD Policy and RAND, enable combinatory approaches to authorities classification. For example, RAND's Security Cooperation Database[4] allows one to sort by program, authority, objective, and purpose (a combination of activity and mission), among other things.[5] Table 3.1 shows one abbreviated entry from this database that relates to the State Department's Africa Contingency Operations Training and Assistance that funds peacekeeping training for African partner security forces.

Pros and Cons of Different Approaches

Each of the aforementioned categorization schemes has advantages and disadvantages with respect to classifying SC authorities.

An activity-based authorities framework provides flexibility and simplicity to DoD planners and providers in the selection of tools to achieve a variety of current and emerging SC objectives. However, it may not provide them with a transparent understanding of which SC

---

[3]   Based on U.S. DoD capstone guidance not available for public release.

[4]   Moroney, Thaler, and Hogler, 2013, p. 113.

[5]   For a description of the RAND security cooperation database, see Moroney, Thaler, and Hogler, 2013.

Table 3.1
Entry from RAND Security Cooperation Database

Program	Authority	Activities	Purposes/ Missions	Objectives
Africa Contingency Operations Training and Assistance	22 U.S.C. Sec. 2348, Peace- keeping Operations: General Authorization	• Training • Confer- ences and workshops • Equipment • Defense and min- istry contacts	• Humanitarian assistance • Port security • Inter- operability • Stabilization and recon- struction • Border security • Maritime security • Disaster relief • Peace- keeping • Coalition operations	Immediate objective: support the establishment of the African Union's African Standby Force/ Brigades by June 2010. Long-term objective: assist the African Union, REC brigades, and individual Troop Contributing Countries in its peacekeeping operations for as long as needed.

resources can or cannot be used in particular circumstances (which is presumably a goal of those in the administration and Congress who oversee the execution of SC activities).

Mission-based schemes potentially provide a good understanding of where, when, how, and under what conditions SC resources can be applied—and they can enable the packaging of resources to achieve particular ends. But this type of classification approach may not provide an enduring or comprehensive framework that would account for a full range of current and emergent SC requirements. Thus, enacting a mission-based authorities structure may encourage SC providers to "game the system" in order to conduct activities that are not clearly connected to an authorized mission but believe are necessary to satisfy SC requirements with respect to key partners.

In contrast, an objective-based approach could provide a comprehensive authorities framework that would not unduly constrain their scope. As indicated above, existing objective categories tend to be broad and overlapping, but they are not always the best way to classify SC efforts that are intended to achieve more than one effect.

Because they classify SC elements by more than one dimension, combinatory approaches can potentially capitalize on the positive aspects of narrower schemes while offsetting their disadvantages. However, they are not particularly helpful unless they indicate which dimension is dominant for classification purposes. In other words, should one categorize authorities first by objective, then by mission and, then by activity—or in some other order?

Hybrid Approach to Categorizing Authorities Has Merit

Given that each classification approach has significant pros and cons, we have chosen to employ a hybrid approach in constructing an authorities framework, which recognizes the descriptive significance of several SC dimensions but further specifies when one or the other should be employed as the main classifier.

Our hybrid framework for organizing SC authorities is based a three guiding principles:
1. create categories that facilitate standardization but also satisfy the requirement for a certain degree of specialization
2. establish a minimum number of categories that cover the dimensions of interest to SC stakeholders
3. develop subcategories associated with dimensional categories that are drawn from existing categorization schemes.

DoD Prefers Standardized Over Specialized Authorities

From our discussions with planners and providers in DoD, it is clear they prefer an authorities framework that is largely organized around the tools they rely on to conduct routine SC activities. These "standardized" authorities could be used in most places, most of the time, with most partners. In other words, they would authorize generic activities that could be carried out as needed with few restrictions as to the mission performed, the objective pursued, or the country engaged.

In addition, because these authorities were meant to be enduring and not time-delimited, they would be placed in the U.S. Code (under Title 10) as permanent statutes. However, DoD stakeholders acknowledge—and congressional stakeholders insist upon—the need for some SC authorities that could only be used in particular circumstances. These "specialized" authorities would be specifically tailored in some way to limit or direct their use—for example, with respect to certain countries, mission areas, or time periods. Not necessarily intended to last for the foreseeable future, they would be expressed in Public Laws, which would have to be reauthorized to continue in effect, rather than being incorporated into the U.S. Code.

Faced with competing imperatives on the part of SC practitioners and oversight agencies—the one to standardize and the other to specialize—we took a balanced approach to restructuring SC authorities. Where there appears to be stakeholder consensus (or at least not significant disagreement) on developing standardized SC tools, we demonstrate how consolidation or expansion of existing legislation might accomplish such restructuring. However, we also allow for specialized authorities in those realms of SC that are complex, sensitive, risky, or unique. Such areas may include current authorities that stakeholders have recommended should remain as they are (i.e., "do no harm") and some new authorities they have proposed based on emergent requirements. For example, relevant DoD stakeholders seem satisfied with current specialized CN legislation. But some responsible for BPC and interoperability in the areas of BMD and cybersecurity have argued for new or expanded SC authority with respect to these particular military missions.

SC Authorities Fit Best Within a Three-Dimensional Framework

In the process of attempting to distinguish among categories of SC authorities, we realized that classifying by activity could be a useful starting point for separating standard from specialized authorities because, at least theoretically, an activity-based authority could be used for any number of purposes. However, after reviewing the gamut of actual SC cooperation authorities, we concluded that they are rarely if ever one-dimensional. While some were primarily activity-based authorities, they usually had other attributes that could be used to categorize them. Furthermore, authorities that did not appear to be primarily activity-based—and, thus, could be considered specialized—could not be placed in a single "bucket" in that they were often specialized in different ways. Consequently, the study team accepted the necessity of a combinatorial approach to classification. But we also sought a method that would enable us to divide SC authorities—whether standard or specialized—into a limited set of clear categories.

Taking into account the alternative approaches to categorizing SC elements described and the characteristics of current SC-related legislation, the study team developed a construct with three basic dimensions that could be used as the basis for classifying existing authorities and developing new ones:

- activity relates to the things that SC practitioners are authorized to do (e.g., provide professional military education to foreign country students)
- mission relates the authorized purposes for which SC practitioners can conduct SC (e.g., to build partner-nation CT capabilities)
- partner relates to the international and foreign partners SC practitioners are authorized to engage. These are usually particular countries (e.g., Ukraine), but they can be multilateral governmental or nongovernmental organizations (e.g., NATO, the United Nations, or the African Union).

A subordinate dimension relates to the period of time SC practitioners are authorized to conduct an activity or a mission with a given partner or partners. Although there are no existing Title 10 statutes that can be characterized as primarily time-based, some DoD personnel, particularly those out in the field, have expressed a need to modify or expand SC authorities to better respond to unforeseen, exigent circumstances for which an important consideration is timeliness—for example, by permitting the distribution of small amounts of equipment and supplies to foreign forces or multilateral organizations involved in ongoing operations through a rapid procurement process or by allowing them to tap into U.S. military stocks or designated regional warehouses. Other stakeholders have suggested that it is DoD systems and processes—which are based on laws and regulations—that get in the way of rapid fielding. Regardless of how the DoD or Congress addresses the time issue, we do not consider time a primary category when evaluating authorities; it is a secondary dimension with varying importance depending on circumstances.

RAND's categorization approach acknowledges the multidimensionality of most SC authorities in theory and practice. At the same time, we posit that most authorities can usefully be distinguished from one another based on a single major dimension. That said, a certain degree of consolidation, clarification, or expansion of the existing set of authorities might be required to fully align them with the structure we are proposing. As Figure 3.1 shows, the authorities found in activity-, mission-, or partner-based categories may have all three primary dimensional characteristics in addition to time, but one dimension is considered dominant for the purpose of classification. In addition, the activity-based category contains mostly standardized authorities that can be employed in a variety of contexts. Mission- and partner-based categories contain authorities that can be employed for different kinds of specialized uses.

Figure 3.1
Three Basic Categories of Authorities

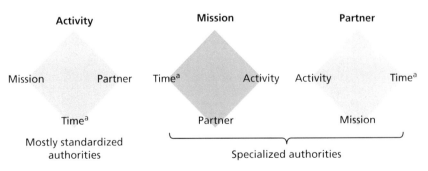

[a] Time is a secondary dimension whose importance is determined by the nature of the authority.

RAND RR1438-3.1

Range and Complexity of Authorities Requires Further Disaggregation

From an examination of the range and complexity of SC legislation, it was evident that a comprehensive classification approach would require linking detailed subcategories to our high-level authorities framework (see Figure 3.2). Fortunately, we were able to draw from previous classification schemes for most of the subcategories related to activities and missions.

As Figure 3.2 shows, our standard set of activity-based authorities includes routine mil-mil engagements, exercises, individual education and technical training, unit train-and-equip activities with established partners, and relatively small-scale research, development, training, and evaluation (RDT&E) programs with U.S. allies. Although listed in the activity category, intelligence sharing and exchange activities are inherently sensitive and can be complex and narrowly tailored. Thus, we consider intelligence sharing as a type of specialized activity subcategory.

Except for intelligence sharing, our specialized subcategories fall within the mission and partner authorities "bins." A number of special-

Figure 3.2
Proposed Categories and Subcategories of Authorities

Activity-Based Authorities
- Mil-mil engagements
- Exercises
- Individual education and technical training
- Unit train and equip
- Equipment and logistics support
- RDT&E
- Intel sharing and exchange

Mission-Based Authorities
- Humanitarian assistance
- Defense institution building
- Counternarcotics
- Cooperative threat reduction and nonproliferation
- Counterterrorism
- Cooperative BMD
- Maritime security
- Cybersecurity

Partner-Based Authorities
- Specific to partners, regions, and organizations

Subcategories of standardized authorities
Subcategories of specialized authorities

ized mission-based SC authorities have been in existence since before 2001. The issue for DoD is deciding—together with the administration and Congress—which missions require separate or additional authorities and which could be dealt with through the application of standard SC mechanisms. Based on our stakeholder discussions, we have concluded that requirements for special authorities will continue to exist for cooperative threat reduction and nonproliferation, CT, CN, DIB, and humanitarian assistance and health (although some consolidation of current authorities may be desirable). Furthermore, new or expanded authorities may be needed for emerging missions, such as cybersecurity, BMD, and maritime security.

Ideally, partner-based authorities would be limited to partners whose relations with the United States are especially sensitive or the engagement risks are exceptionally high. Or they would exist temporarily to meet a short-term requirement that cannot be easily met through the use of current authorities. In reality, the decision on whether to tailor an SC authority to a specific partner is politically determined. That said, partner-based legislation—targeted, for example, to helping Ukraine cope with the insurgency in its eastern provinces or tracking down the Lord's Resistance Army (LRA), in central Africa—could be reviewed every several years and extended, terminated, or, if possible, incorporating related activities under standard SC authorities.

Appendix A categorizes the FY 2015 Title 10 (and Title 22) SC authorities according to our hybrid categorization structure.

Conclusion: Utility of a Hybrid Categorization Structure

Our hybrid structure for categorizing SC authorities according to primary and secondary criteria, representing different elements of SC and indicating different types or degrees of standardization and specialization, can serve a number of useful functions. First, such an authorities framework can provide insight into the relationship between legislative authorities and SC ends, ways, and means by suggesting where they appear to align or where there may be gaps or disconnects. Second, the framework is a practical device for grouping existing authorities that

SC planners and implementers can employ to determine which tools or combination of tools are potentially available to address their particular partner requirements. Third, our framework can assist SC reform advocates seeking to rationalize the current "patchwork" of authorities by furnishing a coherent, flexible, and reality-based mechanism for organizing their legislative proposals.

In line with this last function, the hybrid categorization scheme described in this chapter provides a top-level structure for the next chapter, which offers specific recommendations for modifying and reinforcing the existing set of SC authorities. In particular, the framework subcategories suggest areas in which existing authorities might be consolidated to encompass a wider range of missions or partners or expanded to fill a recognized gap in SC coverage.

CHAPTER FOUR

Rationalizing the Patchwork: Options for Improvement

In this chapter, we follow the framework introduced in Chapter Three to classify Title 10 SC authorities as of FY 2015 and consider potential authority changes to mitigate challenges and meet requirements put forward by DoD and congressional stakeholders.[1]

First, we explain how each of the major SC authorities in Title 10 of the U.S. Code and relevant Public Law can be categorized as activity-, mission-, or partner-based and then divided into subcategories based on their primary purpose. While we do not mention all of the SC-related authorities, the full list of 123 statutes, categorized according to our framework, can be found in Appendix A. It is important to note that the list omits most appropriations and related programs; we refer only to those Title 10 authorities that are codified in U.S. Code or included in authorization legislation, primarily annual National Defense Authorization Acts. In addition, we differentiate what we call "core" authorities from "supporting" authorities in Appendix A. Core authorities are those statutes that directly authorize SC activities, such as training and exercises, and constrain them based on the intent of Congress. Supporting authorities, usually in Public Law, mandate reports or transfers of funds from one account to another, but they do not directly legislate SC activities that DoD can undertake. Core Title 10 authorities are the focus of this report.

---

[1]   Our analysis focuses on statutes that were enacted through FY 2015; however, we do reference several relevant changes to SC authorities in proposed FY 2016 legislation.

Based on these subcategories of authorities, we are able to organize and reference the input from SC personnel in the CCMDs, the military services, OSD, and DoD agencies, as well as from congressional staffers, to gain insight into the utility of the authorities in addressing each particular set of SC activities and missions. The subcategories also enable us to see potential areas of overlap and gaps. For example, there were as many as 23 authorities for individual education and technical training, indicating that there may be areas of overlap in authorities, whereas for ballistic missile defense there were no core Title 10 authorities, reflecting a possible gap.

Next, we focus on the most-prominent changes to authorities suggested in our review of challenges and the hybrid categorization framework. We address four different types of changes to authorities.

- Consolidation: combining similar authorities into one comprehensive or "umbrella" authority
- Revision: amending an existing authority to allow for reasonable improvements in time allowances, flexibility, and ability to engage partners
- Clarification: better illuminating how and when DoD can use certain authorities to eliminate ambiguity in interpretation
- New authority: establishing congressional intent in areas where there are important gaps.

To address potential overlaps, we undertake a winnowing process within each subcategory. First, we consider those authorities that are similar and mentioned by stakeholders as candidates for consolidation. Within the subcategory of mil-mil exchanges, for example, there are authorities regarding the payment of expenses for defense personnel that contain nearly identical language and are used similarly by the CCMDs that may be effectively rolled into a single authority.

Beyond consolidation, we look at those authorities that could be revised to improve their effectiveness. Based on stakeholder input, we consider opportunities for broadening existing language to reasonably expand their scope or applicability. For unit train-and-equip activities, for example, it may be possible to expand the mission of Section 2282,

Authority to Build the Capacity of Foreign Security Forces, beyond CT to focus on emerging threats and allow for the training and equipping of multinational entities. For mil-mil activities, it includes making exchange authorities more global in scope.

Third, we consider sections of the U.S. Code and Public Laws that simply may require clarification as to how and under what circumstances DoD can use certain authorities. For example, DoD personnel at the CCMDs indicated that there was uncertainty over whether Section 168 allowed DoD to support military engagements, which greatly limited its applicability.

We then review areas where stakeholders indicated that there are gaps in existing authorities and a potential need to establish congressional intent for addressing evolving issues of international SC. Such gaps appear to exist in addressing issues of cybersecurity and sustainment.

Finally, we consider a significant number of remaining authorities in each subcategory that did not appear to be good candidates for consolidation, nor in need of revision, clarification, or additional legislation. Many of these sections of the U.S. Code or Public Law are unique in addressing particular areas of SC or especially complex and therefore better left alone. Others were noted to be particularly useful to stakeholders in their present forms and likely would do more harm if they were modified or combined. Still, the stakeholders we engaged did not mention other statutes, and it did not appear that they were using them. However, our study was not scoped to discuss authorities with every SC stakeholder in DoD, so some statutes were not covered. These authorities, which are included in Appendix A, could be considered subject to further investigation.

In sum, our analysis begins with an initial list of 123 Title 10 statutes. Through a review of these statutes, we identify 17 supporting ones that do not directly legislate SC activities with partners and set them aside, leaving 106 core authorities. In the course of our research and discussions with stakeholders, we find that we could consolidate a number of similar authorities and reduce the 106 core authorities by 16 to a total of 90, and we also suggest areas for revision and clarification in several of the remaining 90 authorities. Finally, we propose adding one new authority to address emerging missions. This provides us with a new, streamlined list of 91 core authorities, of which there are 56 activity-based, 22 mission-based, and 13 partner-based authorities. This list can be found in Appendix B.

Review of and Recommended Changes to Existing Title 10 Authorities

Next, we review the existing Title 10 statutes, beginning with an introduction of the four categories of authorities and a brief discussion of the statutes and key issues within each subcategory. Each discussion includes a table summarizing proposed major "muscle movements" in that subcategory, including a list of relevant statutes and recommended changes. We conclude each subcategory section with justifications for these changes.

Activity-Based Authorities

The majority of SC authorities under Title 10 can be categorized as standardized, activity-based statutes. These statutes cover regular interactions with foreign partners in a variety of contexts and generally are not restricted to any particular country or mission. The types of activities that the statutes cover vary. However, as introduced in Chapter Three, the activities can be divided into seven separate subcategories: mil-mil engagements, exercises, individual educational and technical training, unit train and equip, equipment and logistics support, RDT&E, and intelligence sharing and exchange.

Mil-mil engagements between individual U.S. and foreign military personnel are among the most common of the DoD's regular, standardized activities. Currently, there are nine different authorities enabling mil-mil contacts (see Table 4.1). These statutes include Section 168 of U.S. Code that provides the authority to conduct mil-mil contacts and comparable activities; Section 1051 that authorizes the payment of expenses for personnel of developing countries to attend multilateral, bilateral, or regional conferences or seminars; and Section 1051a that provides for support and payment of expenses for personnel from developing countries serving as liaison officers, as well as Section 1203 of Public Law 113-291 that provides enhanced authority for their support. Two additional authorities provide for the payment of expenses of personnel from a particular region: Section 1050 for personnel from Latin America and 1050a for personnel from Africa. And, two authorities exist in Public Law (Public Law 104-201, Section 1082, and Public Law 111-84, Section 1207) that enable the DoD to engage in and provide support for the exchange of defense personnel with foreign countries and nonreciprocal exchanges, respectively.

DoD personnel rely on a combination of these nine authorities to conduct a mil-mil engagement event, which varies according to the participants in each event.[2] As noted in Chapter Two, the balancing of several different authorities has proven to be difficult for SC personnel, as the failure to receive one source of funding can result in the cancelation of a scheduled event. One-year funding also limits continuity in planning and the ability to accommodate changes in foreign partner availability and scheduling delays.[3]

---

[2] Discussions with DoD officials, May 5, 2015, May 7–8, 2015, April 23, 2015, and April 29, 2015.

[3] Discussions with DoD officials, May 7–8, 2015, and October 14, 2015

Table 4.1
Changes to Mil-Mil Engagement Authorities

Authority and Purpose	Suggested Change (Consolidate, Revise, Clarify, New Authority)
10 U.S.C., Sec. 168—Mil-mil Contacts Designed to Encourage Democratic Orientation	• Clarify to identify funding source as O&M, as intended • Clarify that activities "support cooperation and reinforce democratic values" • Revise to incorporate other mil-mil authorities to ensure broad application • Revise to allow more flexible two-year funding
10 U.S.C. Sec. 1050—Payment of Expenses, Defense Personnel, Latin America 10 U.S.C. Sec. 1050a—Payment of Expenses, Defense Personnel, Africa 10 U.S.C. Sec. 1051—Payment of Expenses, Personnel, Developing Countries 10 U.S.C. Sec. 1051a—Expenses for Liaison Officers, Developing Countries Pub. L. 113-291, Sec. 1203—Exchange of Defense Personnel with Foreign Countries	• Consolidate similar mil-mil authorities to make one simpler, global authority available to all CCMDs • Revise to relax determination of "developing country" to ensure consistency of priority engagements • Revise to allow more flexible two-year funding
Pub. L. 104-201, Sec. 1082—Exchange of Defense Personnel with Foreign Countries Pub. L. 111-84, Sec. 1207—Nonreciprocal Exchanges of Defense Personnel	• Consolidate into one authority for personnel exchanges • Revise to allow exchanges with regional organizations to enable multinational interactions

NOTE: This table only reflects authorities in which we suggest changes, not all authorities in this subcategory.

Based on the insight provided by DoD personnel, the first step toward facilitating mil-mil contacts across all of the geographic CCMDs may be to clarify that DoD is permitted to use O&M funds under Section 168 of the U.S. Code and that such use does not require a specific annual appropriation.[4] This clarification would ensure that DoD planners have access to a general funding source for bilateral and multilateral engagements, as Congress originally intended.[5] It also may be beneficial to clarify the purpose of the contacts permitted under Section 168 to ensure that it is not restricted to those "designed to encourage a democratic orientation of defense establishments and military forces" but could include those activities that "support cooperation and reinforce democratic values."[6] Moreover, the authority could be revised and broadened to ensure its availability to support a broad range of mil-mil engagements.

To simplify the current patchwork of mil-mil engagement authorities, it also may be helpful to consolidate the regionally oriented statutes with similar wording—Sections 1050 and 1050a of Title 10 U.S. Code, Latin American and African Cooperation, respectively, as well as the authorities that designate funding for developing countries: Sections 1051 and 1051a of Title 10 U.S. Code and Section 1203 of Public Law 113-291—into one global statute authorizing the payment of personnel expenses for lower-income nations under more flexible metrics of eligibility that are less likely to vary from year to year (e.g., utilizing FMF eligibility criteria). Such an authority could still maintain congressional restrictions on higher-income countries to which assistance should not be provided.

Consolidating these statutes, without regard to geography, would make personnel expenses available across all CCMDs and would encourage cross-CCMD planning. A global authority with more flexible eligibility requirements would also allow for more consistent engagement with developing countries and support regional engagements that are directed at pursuing U.S. security interests. It may also be possible to extend the FY time constraints on mil-mil exchanges

---

[4]   Discussions with DoD officials, April 23, 2015, May 5, 2015, and May 7–8, 2015.

[5]   Discussions with DoD officials, May 7–8, 2015, and discussion with congressional staff members, Washington, D.C., June 5, 2015.

[6]   U.S. Code states that the SecDef may conduct mil-mil contacts and comparable activities that are "designed to encourage a democratic orientation"; however, it is widely interpreted to apply to a broader purpose of supporting SC.

to allow for more flexibility between planning and implementation. Two-year funding could better account for the unpredictability of foreign partner schedules and allow for appropriate repurposing of money when conditions on the ground change. A global authority with more flexible funding would require continued coordination with the State Department and comprehensive annual reporting to Congress.

Two other statutes authorizing the exchange of defense personnel and nonreciprocal exchanges could be combined and broadened to further simplify U.S. mil-mil contacts and offer additional opportunities for engagement. Public Law 104-201, Section 1082, and Public Law 111-84, Section 1207 (recently amended by Public Law 112-239, Section 1202) may be combined into one authority on personnel exchanges that would allow interactions with regional security organizations, as well as individual partner nations. While such a broadening would include stipulations by Congress on the types of organizations that could be included, it would help to address a perceived gap in the DoD's ability to engage with regional, multinational organizations.[7]

One additional authority relating to mil-mil engagements, Public Law 112-239, Section 1275, does not appear to be a candidate for consolidation or revision. This authority is specifically tailored to the United States' participation in the Eurocorps organization and its payment of expenses not only for participating members but also for the operating expenses of the Eurocorps headquarters. Therefore, it would be best to allow the statute to remain as a unique authority until further investigation.

Exercises are another major SC activity in which the DoD engages regularly with partner nations (and is part of its standard toolkit). There are currently six authorities that relate to the conduct of exercises, three of which could be consolidated or revised (see Table 4.2). The broadest of these authorities are Title 10, Section 153, which funds Joint Chiefs of Staff exercises, and Title 10, Section 166a, which provides support for exercises through the Combatant Commander Initiative Fund (CCIF). Section 166a permits combatant commanders to provide funds for a variety of activities, including combined exer-

---

[7]   Discussions with DoD officials, April 23, 2015, and May 5, 2015.

cises, to respond to emergent challenges and unforeseen contingency requirements.[8] DoD personnel across most of the CCMDs commented that they regularly utilize these authorities to conduct exercises with foreign nations.[9]

Title 10, Section 2010 DCCEP is a more narrowly focused statute that authorizes the payment of incremental expenses of a developing country participating in a bilateral or multilateral exercise. This program includes the requirement that the exercises must be undertaken primarily to enhance U.S. security interests and are essential to achieving fundamental objectives. It also stipulates that available funds begin in a FY and end in the following FY. DCCEP is widely used across all CCMDs for those countries that meet the program's income eligibility requirements, most often in combination with other exercise authorities.[10]

A new exercise authority introduced in the 2014 NDAA as Public Law 113-66, Section 1203, permits U.S. GPF to train more comprehensively with friendly foreign forces, requiring only that to the "maximum extent practicable" training aligns with the mission-essential tasks of participating U.S. units and authorizes payment of incremen-

---

[8] CCIF covers a full range of activities, including force training, contingencies, selected operations, command and control, humanitarian and civic assistance, military education and training, personnel expenses of defense personnel for bilateral or regional cooperation programs, force protection, and joint warfighting capabilities, as well as joint exercises and activities of participating foreign countries to enable combatant commanders to respond to emergent challenges and unforeseen contingency requirements. (It is placed under exercises in our categorization because that is where it plays a primary role in SC.)

[9] PACOM does not rely on Section 166a or CCIF to conduct exercises as it has a special Asia-Pacific Regional Initiative program fund that provides funding for this purpose (APRI is authorized though appropriations). Discussions with DoD officials, April 16, 2015, April 23, 2015, April 29, 2015, May 5, 2015, May 7–8, 2015, and October 14, 2015

[10] The statute does not explicitly state the definition of a developing country; however, the DoD has determined an individual country's eligibility through a combination of metrics provided by the World Bank's List of Economies, the International Monetary Fund's World Economic Outlook, and the United Nations Development Program's Human Development Report. Discussions with DoD officials, April 16, 2015, May 5, 2015, May 7–8, 2015, and October 14, 2015.

tal expenses for foreign countries without regard to income.[11] However, in its first year after authorization, the authority was rarely utilized because of difficulties and confusion over procedures for implementation and lack of associated appropriations.[12] Some defense officials have recommended that this authority be incorporated into the DCCEP program to allow broader utilization.[13]

Table 4.2
Changes to Exercise Authorities

Authority and Purpose	Suggested Change (Consolidate, Revise, Clarify, New Authority)
10 U.S.C. Sec. 2010—Payment of Incremental Expenses for Developing Countries to Participate in Combined Exercises Pub. L. 113-66, Sec. 1203—Training of General Purpose Forces of the U.S. Armed Forces with Military and Other Security Forces of Friendly Foreign Countries	• Revise to relax determination of "developing country" to ensure consistency and facilitate regional cooperation • Consolidate to become single authority for supporting partner-nation participation in exercises to eliminate income requirements and enable "Big T" training
10 U.S.C. Sec. 2805— Unspecified Minor Construction	• Revise to allow more flexible, two-year funding

NOTE: This table only reflects authorities in which we suggest changes, not all authorities in this subcategory.

---

[11] The statute authorizes training that supports to the maximum extent practicable the mission-essential tasks for which the training unit providing such training is responsible, with a foreign unit with equipment that is functionally similar to such a training unit, and includes elements that promote respect for human rights and legitimate civilian authority within the foreign country. It also authorizes the payment of incremental expenses incurred by a friendly foreign country as the direct result of training.

[12] Discussions with DoD officials, April 23, 2015, May 5, 2015, May 7–8, 2015, and October 14, 2015.

[13] Discussion with DoD officials, May 5, 2015.

On the other hand, Title 10, Section 2011 JCET, which authorizes U.S. SOF training with foreign forces and is nearly identical to the newer Section 1203, has been heavily used to conduct exercises. Congress authorizes JCETs for the "primary purpose of training U.S. special operations forces of the combatant command," interpreted as meaning that training of foreign forces is secondary or "incidental." They have been employed effectively to provide secondary training to foreign forces—and are thus seen as a SC tool—and to maintain persistent SOF engagements in regions of importance to U.S. national security.[14] As a result, U.S. Special Operations Command (SOCOM) officials have supported maintaining this authority as is and not consolidating it with other authorities like Section 1203. This position is based in large part on SOCOM's need to preserve flexibility and autonomy over the training of special operations forces. However, other DoD officials have indicated that this autonomy often can be at the expense of ensuring that SOCOM's SC activities are aligned with broader SC strategic objectives and other SC activities. Some DoD officials recommend exploring ways to align JCETs with the new Section 1203 exercises to provide greater coordination in achieving broader strategic objectives.[15] JCETs are certainly important for both U.S. training requirements and SC objectives at the technical and strategic levels; the proper balance between them is an area for further investigation.

A sixth statute, Title 10, Section 2805, Unspecified Minor Construction, is often utilized in combination with other exercise authorities, through the Exercise-Related Construction Program.[16] Section 2805 establishes spending limits and reporting requirements for unspecified construction projects and limits O&M funding to $1 million for any one project. Although the statute does not explicitly state

---

[14] Section 2011 of U.S. Code Title 10 also authorizes the payment of expenses of training special operations forces and incremental expenses incurred by developing countries engaged in training.

[15] Discussions with DoD officials, September 3, 2015, and September 23, 2015.

[16] Section 2805 provides general authority for unspecified related construction. The Exercise-Related Construction program is linked to this authority, yet funded through congressional appropriations legislation.

that construction can be for the benefit of foreign forces, it is often used to enhance SC activities.[17] Some officials expressed that such spending limits were too low and that one-year expenditure requirements restrict its utility.

The existing list of exercise-related statutes can undergo some consolidations, as well as revision to improve their utility. To enable DoD personnel to engage additional lower-income countries in combined and multilateral exercises, it may be possible to revise the metrics used to determine which countries are eligible to receive payment for incremental expenses.[18] Introducing more flexible eligibility measures could improve the consistency of U.S. engagements and facilitate more regional cooperation. It may also be reasonable to consider consolidating the relatively new Section 1203 statute with DCCEP to create a single authority for the support of partner-nation participation in exercises and training. Such a consolidation would eliminate income requirements for partner-nation participation and may allow for more broad-based exercises that would enable partner nations to develop new capabilities, as some interpret Section 1203 as allowing "Big T training," or training to improve the capacity of foreign forces beyond minimal level necessary to achieve interoperability, safety, or familiarization with U.S. forces in preparing for combined military operations.[19] It would not, however, provide additional funding, as neither authority includes designated appropriations, but rely on O&M funds. It may require the removal of funding caps established for each authority.

---

[17] Discussions with DoD officials, April 23, 2015, April 29, 2015, and October 14, 2015.

[18] One option, as mentioned for Section 1051, would enable all countries eligible for FMF to receive DCCEP funding. Another option would be for DoD to change the metrics it uses to define a developing country.

[19] DoD training with foreign forces is generally restricted to the purposes of interoperability, safety, and familiarization for U.S. forces, or "little t" training. However, the legislative proposal for the FY 2014 NDAA reportedly included the stipulation that training under Section 1203 could have the dual benefit of improving U.S. military relationships with and the military capacity of allied forces. However, some DoD officials at the CCMDs do not believe that such "Big T" training is authorized. Ryan W. Leary, "A Big Change to Limitations on 'Big T' Training: The New Authority to Conduct Security Assistance Training with Allied Forces," *The Army Lawyer*, February 2014; discussion with DoD officials, May 5, 2015.

Minor construction authority could be reviewed to allow more flexibility in FY spending requirements to enable the DoD to complete construction projects necessary to engage in more complex partner-nation exercises and to accommodate delays in the ordering and delivery of equipment.

The remaining exercise authorities would not require any changes. The CCIF under Section 166a is a broad authority that encompasses a wide range of activities beyond exercises, whereas Section 2011 is unique to U.S. SOF training and is effective in its current form.[20] However, as noted earlier, there is disagreement within DoD over the need to maintain Section 2011 as a separate authority as opposed to consolidating it with Sections 2010 and 1203 as an overarching exercise authority for SOF and GPF.[21]

Individual education and technical training is a third major subcategory of SC activities that includes a total of 23 authorities. Many of these statutes contain similar but military service–specific language under separate sections of U.S. Code. There are three nearly identical sections of U.S. Code that focus on foreign personnel attending military academies: Section 4344, Selection of Foreign Cadets Attending the Military Academy; Section 6957, Foreign Midshipmen Attending the Naval Academy; and Section 9344, Selection of Persons from Foreign Countries, the Air Force Academy. Likewise, there are seven common statutes that regulate academic and cultural exchange programs between U.S. and foreign military academies (see Table 4.3). DoD personnel did not indicate that they had any difficulty utilizing these authorities in their current form; however, they appear to demonstrate redundancy in the U.S. Code.[22]

---

[20] Discussions with DoD officials, April 23, 2015, May 5, 2015, and May 6, 2015.

[21] Discussion with DoD officials, July 3, 2015.

[22] Discussions with DoD officials, April 16, 2015, April 23, 2015, April 29, 2015, May 5, 2015, May 7–8, 2015, and October 14, 2015.

Table 4.3 Changes to Individual Education and Technical Training Authorities

Authority and Purpose	Suggested Change (Consolidate, Revise, Clarify, New Authority)
10 U.S.C. Sec. 4344—Foreign Cadets Attending the Military Academy 10 U.S.C. Sec. 6957—Foreign Midshipmen Attending the Naval Academy 10 U.S.C. Sec. 9344—Selection of Persons from Foreign Countries, Air Force Academy	Consolidate similar authorities to provide single authority for use by each service academy to select international students to improve bureaucratic efficiency
10 U.S.C. Sec. 4345—Military Academy Exchange Program 10 U.S.C. Sec. 4345a—Military Academy Cultural Exchange 10 U.S.C. Sec. 6957a—Naval Academy Exchange Program 10 U.S.C. Sec. 6957b—Navy Academy Cultural Exchange 10 U.S.C. Sec. 9345—Air Force Academy Exchange 10 U.S.C. Sec. 9345a—Air Force Academy Cultural Exchange Pub. L. 113-291, Sec. 5530—Duration of Exchange Activities at Military Service Academies	Consolidate similar authorities to provide single authority for use by each service academy to conduct exchange programs and improve bureaucratic efficiency
10 U.S.C. Sec. 2249c— Regional Defense Combating Terrorism Fellowship Program (CTFP)	Revise to enable CTFP to adopt broader mission of "emerging threats"

NOTE: This table only reflects authorities in which we suggest changes, not all authorities in this subcategory.

A number of defense officials specifically mentioned Section 2249c of the U.S. Code, which established the Regional Defense Combating Terrorism Fellowship Program (CTFP) for the education and

Training of foreign officials.[23] This program was noted in Chapter Two as being a successful program, but it has been limited to counterterrorism issues.[24] The remaining 12 education and technical training statutes include authorities that establish special schoolhouses, such as the Inter-American Air Forces Academy (Section 9415), regional centers for security studies (Section 184), and military centers of excellence (Section 2350m). Others stipulate the eligibility for such programs as the Senior Reserve Officers' Training Corps (Section 2103) and the distribution of education and training materials to foreign personnel (Section 2249d). While numerous, there was no indication that these particular authorities were posing any difficulty.[25]

Congress could consolidate the three education authorities that contain nearly identical language regarding the selection and funding of foreign personnel attending military academies to simplify this subcategory. In addition, there are six similarly worded statutes authorizing military exchange programs and cultural exchanges with foreign military forces that could be combined, and an associated amendment regarding the duration of exchange activities also could be included. The consolidation of these authorities would reduce the number of duplicative statutes, as well as decrease the volume of cable traffic between DoD personnel and help to improve the efficiency of the bureaucracy involved in implementing educational and cultural exchange activities.

Broadening the CTFP's scope to include emerging threats could expand its effectiveness and utility. This would enable DoD to apply the success the program has had in CT to new areas of concern such

---

[23] Discussion with DoD officials, April 23, 2015.

[24] The CTFP was designed to strengthen the institutional counterterrorism capacity of key defense and security officials of partner nations through strategic and operational level education and training, focusing on terrorists' methodologies and the mix of direct and indirect ways and means to counter them. It has become the "go to" program within DoD to train international security personnel to combat terrorism. James Miller, "DoD Policy and Responsibilities Relating to the Regional Defense Combating Terrorism Fellowship Program (CTFP)," instructional memorandum DoDI 2000.28, Office of the Under Secretary of Defense for Policy, U.S. Department of Defense, November 14, 2013.

[25] Discussions with DoD officials, April 16, 2015, April 23, 2015, April 29, 2015, May 5, 2015, May 7–8, 2015, and October 14, 2015.

as cybersecurity, which could benefit from greater cooperation with foreign partners.

Among the remaining education authorities, there is less overlap or room for expansion. They include unique authorities that focus on one particular area or the establishment of a special entity, such as the Aviation Leadership Program, and are not good candidates for consolidation or revision.

Unit train and equip is a subcategory of SC activities that has grown in significance to the DoD over the last decade. While the DoD traditionally has engaged in training and equipping through Title 22 programs (such as FMF and FMS), the SecDef was given the authority to train and equip foreign military forces—specifically for CT and stability operations—with the passage of Section 1206 of Public Law 109-163 in 2005.[26] This new authority was intended to provide a flexible funding mechanism to enable CCMDs to respond rapidly to emergent threats. It was extended annually through 2014 and subsequently became codified under Section 2282 of the U.S. Code, which included an expanded authority to build the capacity of a foreign country's maritime, border security, or other national-level security forces to conduct CT operations. Section 2282 and its 1206 predecessor have been used extensively in CENTCOM, AFRICOM, EUCOM, and, until recently, PACOM (see Table 4.4).[27]

A second train-and-equip authority, the GSCF, was introduced in 2011 in Public Law 112-81, Section 1207, to address some of the concerns about the effectiveness and flexibility of Section 1206, outlined in Chapter Two. GSCF was established as a four-year pilot project to be jointly administered and funded by DoD and DoS to carry out security and counterterrorism training and rule of law programs.[28] As indicated in Chapter Two, however, complicated process requirements

---

[26] Section 1206 was established as a "dual-key" program that required both the DoD and the Department of State to approve train-and-equip proposals and expenditures.

[27] Discussions with DoD officials, April 16, 2015, April 23, 2015, April 29, 2015, May 5, 2015, May 7–8, 2015, and October 14, 2015.

[28] Nina M. Serafino, *Global Security Contingency Fund: Summary and Issue Overview*, Washington, D.C.: Congressional Research Service, R42641, April 4, 2014.

and lack of associated appropriations have severely limited utilization of the authority.[29]

Two other Title 10 authorities that have a train-and-equip component include Section 408(c) of U.S. Code, which authorizes the provision of equipment and training to foreign personnel to assist in the DoD in accounting for missing U.S. government personnel, and Public Law 110-417, Section 943 (as amended by Public Law 113-291, Section 126), which authorizes nonconventional assisted recovery capabilities, including the provision of limited amounts of equipment, training, and logistical support. These authorities are far more limited in scope than Section 2282 or 1207 and were not mentioned by DoD personnel as being utilized or in need of revision.[30]

Some revisions to the current 2282 authority could improve the utility and effectiveness of U.S. training and equipping efforts. Based on stakeholders' comments, it would be beneficial to expand the mission set of 2282 beyond counterterrorism and stability operations to enable U.S. foreign partners to address emerging threats, such as hybrid warfare. It would also be helpful to address emerging threats that transcend national boundaries by permitting U.S. forces to train multinational or regional entities. Also, it may be advisable to include a clarification to Section 2282 that allows the DoD to train and equip foreign

---

[29] The GSCF authority permits DoD and the State Department to transfer up to $250 million from other accounts, with a limit of $200 million from DoD and $50 million from State to facilitate SC activities, yet it does not include new money for the fund, nor was additional money provided in subsequent appropriations legislation (Serafino, 2014); and discussions with DoD officials, April 16, 2015, April 23, 2015, April 29, 2015, May 5, 2015, May 7–8, 2015, and October 14, 2015.

[30] Discussions with DoD officials, April 16, 2015, April 23, 2015, April 29, 2015, May 5, 2015, May 7–8, 2015, and October 14, 2015. A fifth statute, Public Law 112-239, Section 1532, which established the Joint Improvised Explosive Device Defeat fund, authorized training, equipment, supplies, and services to Pakistan to counter IEDs. However, it is not clear if this train-and-equip authority will be utilized subsequent to the merging of the JIEDO organization into the broader Joint-Improvised Threat Defeat Agency within the Office of the Undersecretary of Defense for Acquisition, Technology & Logistics in May 2015. Therefore, we decided to not to include this statute in the unit train-and-equip authority. Joint Improvised-Threat Defeat Agency, *About JIDA*, web page, undated; and Marcus Weisgerber, "Pentagon's IED Office Reinvents Itself for a New War," *Defense One*, July 13, 2015.

Table 4.4
Changes to Unit Train-and-Equip Authorities

Authority and Purpose	Suggested Change (Consolidate, Revise, Clarify, New Authority)
10 U.S.C. Sec. 2282—Training and Equipping of Forces for Counterterrorism and Coalition Operations	• Revise to broaden mission set beyond counterterrorism to address emerging threats • Revise to allow T&E of multinational entities to improve capacity of regional organizations • Revise to relax obligation and funding timelines • Revise to incorporate sustainment plan when intended • Revise to incorporate the most useful aspects of Section 1207 GSCF, including: the authority to train noncounterterrorism units, assist the justice sector, and conduct rule of law programs

NOTE: This table only reflects authorities in which we suggest changes, not all authorities in this subcategory.

partner and regional organizations facing particular sets of threats, as agreed upon by Congress, State, and DoD. Some congressional staff believe that the statute does not restrict U.S. forces to training for the purposes of counterterrorism and stability operations.[31]

To allow for more consistency in planning and better coordination in the provision of equipment and training under Section 2282, it would help to relax fiscal obligations and timelines to allow funding to be dispersed over a three-year timeline (currently 2282 is considered to be a two-year program). At the same time, maintenance plans should be incorporated into U.S. train-and-equip efforts, when the United States and the partner have a vested interest in sustaining the partner's capability over the longer term. In those cases where sustainment is a priority, train-and-equip engagements may include incentives to partners to assume responsibility for sustainment in part by making further assistance contingent on their cooperation in ensuring operational readiness. Reporting requirements under Section 2282 would likely

---

[31] RAND workshop, Washington, D.C., July 17, 2015.

need to be strengthened as well, to ensure that DoD engagements are closely coordinated with DoS and that Congress receives adequate assessments on the progress of ongoing train-and-equip programs to maintain necessary oversight.

More generally, we are not suggesting that a new and separate sustainment authority be enacted. Long-term sustainment of Title 10 programs should be a consideration when planning train-and-equip initiatives. Those initiatives where sustainment is necessary to support high-priority U.S. national security interests should be identified and sources of funding for maintenance, spare parts, and training should be defined during the planning process. Such sources could be partner-country national funds or, secondarily, other U.S. sustainment and/or loan and grant programs.

Given the many difficulties faced in implementing the GSCF, it may not be necessary to extend the authority beyond its initial four-year pilot period. The complicated procedural and concurrence requirements may not be warranted. Yet, there are some aspects of GSCF that DoD stakeholders indicated were valuable and could be incorporated into Section 2282, such as the authority to train non-CT units, to assist the justice sector, and to conduct rule of law programs. Other parts of the GSCF authority stakeholders found problematic—such as its existence as a transfer authority, the requirement that DoD and DoS contribute 80 percent and 20 percent of expenditures, respectively, and a lack of designated appropriations—would not be carried over.

As noted, the other two statutes that include train-and-equip authority, Sections 408(c) and 943, are unique and not easily consolidated.

The subcategory of *equipment and logistics support* encompasses a broader range of statutes that authorize DoD to provide or acquire equipment, logistical supplies, or services to and from foreign nations. It includes a "global lift and sustain" authority (Section 127d of the U.S. Code) that allows DoD to provide logistical support to foreign nations participating in combined operations, as well as specific lift and sustain authorizations in Public Law that permit logistical support for coalition forces supporting operations in Iraq and Afghanistan, including Public Law 110-181, Section 1234 (see Table 4.5). It also includes statutes that authorize the DoD to negotiate acquisition and cross-servicing agreements (ACSAs) and cooperative logistical support arrangements with coalition partners to support U.S. forces deployed abroad. Moreover, there are a number of statues in this sub-category that provide the authority for DoD to provide equipment to other nations through such mechanisms as the lease of non-excess property and the provision of surplus war material to foreign nations.

To begin to streamline the existing set of 21 core equipping and logistics authorities, it may be possible to consolidate the global lift and sustain authority with those similar authorities that are designated to support certain U.S. operations. Although not specifically prohibited in the statute, practitioners were reluctant to use global lift and sustain for coalition support for Afghanistan due to existence of a special lift and sustain authority for that country.[32] It is likely that Congress would want to maintain the ability to target U.S. logistical support to a specific country or coalition of countries through annual appropriations; however, it may not be necessary to enact separate core authorities for logistic support for each operation or region in which the U.S. is engaged.[33]

Consolidation could enable the United States to provide more-comprehensive support to partner nations participating in combined and coalition operations. In addition, it could help alleviate the difficulty DoD planners face in cobbling together a variety of authorities and programs to provide partner nations with training and equipment to ensure interoperability, transport units to theater, sustain them in combat, and redeploy them after their mission has ended. With only one global authority, the DoD may utilize its resources more effectively and respond more quickly when it is directed to provide logistical support to future coalition partners.

---

[32] Contract and Fiscal Law Department, 2014.

[33] Section 1207 of the FY 2016 NDAA authorizes the DoD to "provide support to national military forces of allied countries for counterterrorism operations in Africa." This authority is more narrowly focused than the Global Lift and Sustain authority, as it is specifically targeted to CT operations in Africa and does not require countries to be participating in combined operations.

Table 4.5

Changes to Equipment and Logistics Support Authorities

Authority and Purpose	Suggested Change (Consolidate, Revise, Clarify, New Authority)
10 U.S.C. Sec. 127d—Logistics Support for Allies in Combined Operations (Global Lift and Sustain) Pub. L. 110-181, Sec. 1234— Logistical Support for Coalition Forces Afghanistan/Iraq	Consolidate similar temporary authorities for coalition ops in Afghanistan and Iraq with global lift and sustain authority to improve efficiency and provide more comprehensive global support

NOTE: This table only reflects authorities in which we suggest changes, not all authorities in this subcategory.

Other logistics-related statutes that were written specifically to support the wars in Afghanistan and Iraq—for example, Public Law 109-163, Section 1208, Coalition Support Fund (CSF), which provides reimbursement to countries for expenses incurred while providing logistical and military support to U.S. military operations in Operation Enduring Freedom and Operation Iraqi Freedom, and a program supported by CSF, the CRSP, which enables DoD to provide training, supplies, and equipment to coalition forces (primarily Eastern European forces) engaged in those operations—may have limited applicability in regions where the United States does not have a major force presence, but they could be consolidated and placed within the category of mission-based activities. The statutes may not need to be applied to other countries or regions and could be allowed to expire at the conclusion of U.S. operations in Afghanistan and Iraq. A more-recently enacted statute, Public Law 113-291, Section 1210, which authorizes the DoD to transport certain defense articles from Afghanistan to other countries, may not be relevant after U.S. forces complete their departure from the country.

ACSAs and logistical support agreements with foreign partners in support of U.S. forces include an exceedingly complex set of authorities that have expanded gradually over time. These authorities, which include Title 10 Sections 2341 and 2342, 2350d, and 2350f, were restricted initially to NATO allies, then expanded in the 1980s to include non-NATO nations, such as Japan, Australia, Korea, Israel, and Egypt. Geographical restrictions were lifted in the 1990s, yet significant constraints remain over the type of equipment, munitions, and services that may be exchanged. It may be possible to expand existing ACSA authorities for the United States to provide logistical support to new partners in response to emerging threats. However, given the complexity of these authorities and potential risks changes would entail, any specific changes to the existing ACSA and logistical support authorities for U.S. forces will require further analysis.

It is also important to note that additional analysis is necessary to adopt appropriate reporting requirements for all SC Title 10 statutes, not only complex logistics and support authorities. Public Law 113-291, Section 1211, introduced more significant reporting requirements for a biennial report on DoD programs involving training, equipment, other assistance, and reimbursement to foreign forces, by country, which would include a program's purpose and an explanation of how each advances theater SC strategy, as well as cost and metrics of assessment and any reimbursement provided.[34] As mentioned in Chapter Two, more could be done to align reporting requirements for the benefit of DoD personnel and congressional staffers.

Other authorities in this subcategory that relate to specific mechanisms for transferring equipment to foreign nations appear to be unique and may also require further analysis to determine their utility and whether they could be combined or retired. One particular statute, Section 1276 of Public Law 112-239 that authorizes DoD to participate in a European program on multilateral exchange of air transportation and air refueling services—known as the Air Transport, Air-to-Air Refueling and Other Exchange of Services (ATARES)—stands out as inherently complex and can only be used in particular circumstances. In this case, the program is tailored to certain Euro-

---

[34] The reporting requirement introduced in Section 1211 applies not only to the Global Lift and Sustain program (Section 127d) but also specifies 13 other statutes authorizing DoD to train, equip, assist, or reimburse foreign security forces.

pean member nations who agree to participate in an exchange system of credits and debits to facilitate sharing of Air Force–related activities. It would likely remain "as is" without consolidation or revision until further investigation is completed.

Research, development, test, and evaluation (RDT&E), the sixth major subcategory of SC activities, contains a series of six authorities that allow for cooperative research engagements with foreign partners. These authorities, all of which have been codified in Title 10, include "cooperative research and development agreements" and "defense memoranda of understanding and related agreements" that allow DoD to participate in information exchanges, foreign cooperative testing, research and development programs, and international trade shows and armaments exchanges. These authorities are centrally managed by the Office of the Under Secretary of Defense for Acquisition, Technology, and Logistics and are generally not implemented by the CCMDs. RDT&E statutes were rarely referenced in our discussions with stakeholders and pose little risk of overlap with other SC authorities. Therefore, there does not appear to be any basis to consider changing any of these unique authorities without further research.

RDT&E activities also encompass specialized authorities that involve particularly large, complex weapons systems being developed on a cooperative basis. For example, the Arrow missile system developed with Israel was supported in its early development by RDT&E International Cooperative Program authorities. Similarly, the International Cooperative Program has supported cooperative development of the Standard Missile-3 Block IIA ship-based missile with Japan. Future RDT&E cooperative agreement authorities may be required for the development of other large-scale weapons systems that have a strategic impact on U.S. national security. It should be noted, however, that the development of major weapons systems with foreign partners often goes beyond RDT&E to include acquisition and test and evaluation, as well as joint training activities. While we include this under RDT&E, it is certainly possible to consider the creation of a separate subcategory of SC authorities for large-scale weapons systems that are significantly more complex and costly than traditional RDT&E agreements or other security assistance arrangements.

Intelligence sharing and exchange is the final subcategory of activity-based authorities. It contains three statutes, all in U.S. Code, that may be referred to as specialized (rather than standardized) authorities, as they are inherently sensitive and complex, and are generally tailored in some way to limit their use. One of the three statutes, Section 421 "Intelligence sharing specific to cryptologic support," covers highly classified material and is required to meet special reporting rules under Title 50 authorities. Section 443 focuses on "Imagery intelligence and geospatial information." It provides narrow authority to the National Geospatial-Intelligence Agency to provide imagery intelligence to foreign countries. The third authority, Section 454, is further tailored to permit the SecDef to authorize the National Geospatial-Intelligence Agency to exchange or furnish mapping data. There does not appear to be any basis for these three highly specialized authorities to be consolidated or changed.

Mission-Based Authorities

In addition to the statutes that authorize DoD to undertake SC activities on a routine basis with foreign forces, there are a number of specialized statutes Congress has enacted over the last decade that authorize the U.S. military to engage in SC activities for a specific purpose or mission. These mission-based authorities, both in the U.S. Code and Public Law, have evolved to respond to particular security threats that transcend national borders. Several authorities currently focus on long-standing missions such as humanitarian assistance, CN, nonproliferation, and cooperative threat reduction; there are far fewer authorities that address emerging threats, such as missions like maritime and cybersecurity.

Humanitarian assistance has become an important SC mission for the DoD in the past decade. There are currently eight sections of U.S. Code that authorize the engagement with foreign forces in response to humanitarian disasters (see Table 4.6). Each focuses on a different aspect of DoD's disaster response and training. Section 2561 authorizes the transportation of relief supplies; Section 401 provides for humanitarian and civic assistance during military operations; Section 402 allows for the transportation of the supplies of nongovernmental organizations; Section 404 authorizes engagement in disaster assistance, including transportation, supplies, services, and equipment; Section 2649 enables the transport of civilian and commercial cargo, and Section 2557 allows for the donation of excess nonlethal supplies. Section 407 focuses more narrowly on assistance with humanitarian demining and stockpiled conventional munitions.

According to DoD personnel, each of these humanitarian assistance authorities is utilized in the administration of humanitarian assistance and preparation and planning for disasters by various directorates at the CCMDs.[35] In most CCMDs, the J4 logistics directorate coordinates the transportation of relief supplies, while the J5/8, Policy, Strategy, Partnering and Capabilities directorate, oversees all humanitarian assistance engagement and training efforts.[36] On a broader level, some authorities are overseen and funded by DSCA while OSD and the Joint Staff oversee others.

Further consideration is necessary to determine whether the existing humanitarian authorities could be consolidated without impeding the DoD's ability to respond to various types of disasters.[37] It may be possible, regardless, to revise the authorities so that they are better aligned and more centrally managed. Closer coordination of Sections 2561, 401, 402, 404 and 2557 would allow for more effective use of DoD assets. Interestingly, all of these authorities are at least partially funded by the Defense Security Cooperation Agency (DSCA) administered Overseas Humanitarian, Disaster, and Civic Aid (OHDACA) program and already require DoS approval. Section 401 is funded by both OHDACA and O&M funds. It requires the Secretary of State's approval, while Sections 402 and 407 merely require the Secretary's concurrence. The FY 2016 NDAA links all five of these humanitarian assistance authorities, as well as 407, in legislation requiring program monitoring and evaluation. Those humanitarian assistance authorities

---

[35] Discussions with DoD officials, April 29, 2015, May 7–8, 2015, and October 14, 2015.

[36] Discussions with DoD officials, April 29, 2015, May 7–8, 2015, and October 14, 2015.

[37] 10 U.S.C. Section 2561, for example, authorizes the transportation of humanitarian relief and other humanitarian purposes worldwide, which provides the DoD with the agility to respond to a wide range of disasters.

Table 4.6
Changes to Humanitarian Assistance Authorities

Authority and Purpose	Suggested Change (Consolidate, Revise, Clarify, New Authority)
10 U.S.C. Sec. 2561—Transportation of Relief Supplies 10 U.S.C. Sec. 401—Humanitarian and Civic Assistance During Military Operations 10 U.S.C. Sec. 402—Transportation of Nongovernmental Supplies 10 U.S.C. Sec. 404—Disaster Assistance: Transportation, Supplies, Services, and Equipment 10 U.S.C. Sec. 2649—Transport of Civilian/Commercial Cargo 10 U.S.C. Sec. 2557—Excess Nonlethal Supplies	Revise humanitarian assistance authorities to better align them to improve coordination of DoD assets and funding

NOTE: This table only reflects authorities in which we suggest changes, not all authorities in this subcategory.

that are more unique, such as Sections 407 and 182, are less likely to require revision.

Defense institution building (DIB) is a relatively new form of SC engagement that has recently been introduced though Public Law. This subcategory of activities contains four core authorities. The authority to assign "civilian advisors to foreign ministries of defense," known as the Ministry of Defense Advisors (MODA) program, was enacted in Public Law 112-81, Section 1081. The authority to assign civilian advisers to "regional organizations with security missions" was enacted as an amendment to the MODA program in Public Law 113-291, Section 1047 (see Table 4.7). These authorities enable DoD civilian personnel to deploy to foreign nations and regional security organizations to assist their counterparts in improving their ministerial capacity. While initially developed in response to operational requirements in Afghanistan, the MODA program authorized by Sections 1081 and 1047 is global, with no geographical restrictions. Additionally, Public

Table 4.7
Changes to Defense Institution Building Authorities

Authority and Purpose	Suggested Change (Consolidate, Revise, Clarify, New Authority)
Pub. L. 112-81, Sec. 1081—Assignment of DoD Civilian Advisers to Foreign Ministries of Defense	Revise to also allow U.S. military advisers to be assigned where appropriate
Pub. L. 113-291, Sec. 1047—Assignment of Advisers to Regional Organizations	
Pub. L. 114-92, Sec. 1055—Authority to Provide Training and Support to Personnel of Foreign Ministries of Defense	

NOTE: This table only reflects authorities in which we suggest changes, not all authorities in this subcategory.

Law 113-291, Section 1206, allows DoD personnel to conduct training in foreign security ministries to promote respect for the rule of law and human rights.

MODA authorities have enabled U.S. advisers to become embedded in the MoDs of several countries to assist senior foreign military personnel in defense planning, programming, and budgeting. A fourth authority, Public Law 114-92, Section 1055, authorizes U.S. civilian advisers to provide training to personnel operating below the ministerial level in foreign ministries of defense and regional organizations. This authority allows U.S. advisers to provide assistance in areas of administration and logistics and enables DoD to provide assistance in building key ministry functions in developing countries that request U.S. assistance. Because some U.S. expertise in logistics and other areas resides in the military services, we recommend revising these authorities to permit assignment of U.S. military advisers, as well when this is appropriate.

Counternarcotics is another major mission area for SC. The DoD's authority to engage with foreign forces to combat drug trafficking is derived from four statutes in Public Law that were introduced from 1990 through 2004 and subsequently reauthorized and expanded. Each of these statutes focuses on a particular aspect of counternarcotics activity or a particular group of nations. Section 1004, Support for Counter-Drug Activities, first introduced in Public Law 101-510, authorizes DoD to provide assistance and training for foreign security forces, including foreign police forces. Public Law 105-85, Section 1033, permits DoD to assist certain countries' CN efforts by providing nonlethal protective and utility personnel equipment (originally enacted to help the governments of Peru and Colombia, the authority has expanded through amendments to include 35 countries); Public Law 108-375, Section 1021, authorizes the DoD to support Colombia's unified counterdrug and CT campaign; and Public Law 108-136, Section 1022, permits a DoD joint task force to provide support to law enforcement agencies conducting CT activities, later expanded to include counter-transnational organized crime activities.

All four statutes have been utilized extensively to carry out DoD's CN mission, which supports both partner-nation engagement and U.S. military operational requirements, and includes engagement with both foreign military and police forces. The combination of the existing CN statutes appears to provide the DoD with the necessary authority and flexibility to carry out this unique mission. There is no indication that an attempt to consolidate or revise these authorities would be beneficial (and could indeed cause harm).[38] SC practitioners appear to agree that the flexibility and autonomy in CN authorities strike the right balance in legislation, and they are satisfied with the CN authorities as written. Any consideration of revision, consolidation, or other change would require further investigation.

---

[38] Discussions with DoD officials, April 23, 2015, and April 29, 2015.

Cooperative threat reduction and nonproliferation are activities that DoD has focused on since 1991, primarily through DoS and intelligence authorities. The cooperative threat reduction program (known as the Nunn-Lugar) was initially introduced to provide nonproliferation assistance to Russia, Ukraine, and Kazakhstan to prevent the spread of weapons of mass destruction (WMD) from the former Soviet Union. The program was maintained through subsequent legislation and expanded beyond the states of the former Soviet Union in the 2004 NDAA (Public Law 108-136)—specifically to Asia and the Middle East in Public Law 110-181, Section 1306, which addressed the proliferation of nuclear, chemical, and biological materials. Most of these authorities were later codified as Title 22 and Title 50.

In 2013, however, DoD was provided authority under Title 10 "to conduct activities to enhance the capability of foreign countries to respond to incidents involving weapons of mass destruction" in Public Law 113-66, Section 1204. This statute enables the SecDef to provide assistance to countries bordering Syria to enhance their capability to respond to incidents involving WMD. This statute as well as a subsequent "authority to carry out DoD Cooperative Threat Reduction Program," enacted under Public Law 113-291, Section 1321, have enabled the DoD to use O&M funding to train, equip, and exercise both military and civilian first responders in the states surrounding Syria, namely Jordan, Turkey, Lebanon, and Iraq, and may be expanded to other countries.

DoD officials familiar with this new nonproliferation program indicate that it has been utilized effectively to respond to the emerging threat along Syria's borders.[39] Although there was some indication that other countries would like to receive similar assistance, there is no indication that the current statute should be revised or that a new authority should be introduced.

The Cooperative Threat Reduction Program, which operates under a combination of foreign assistance, intelligence, and defense statutes, is uniquely complex. It is also beyond the scope of our study to recommend revisions for Title 22 or Title 50 authorities. As a new

---

[39] Discussion with DoD officials, April 23, 2015.

Title 10 authority that appears to be operating effectively, no changes are advised at this time.

As noted in Chapter Two, **counterterrorism** has been a major focus of DoD engagements since 2001. Congress introduced a number of Title 10 authorities to address the threat of global terrorism from 2001 through 2015; however, there are few authorities that may be considered mission-oriented. The majority of these authorities have been focused on particular activities, such as Sections 1206 and 2282 Train and Equip Programs, or particular countries or partners—namely, Afghanistan, Iraq, Pakistan, and Syria—or introduced through appropriations (as opposed to authorization) legislation, such as the Trans-Sahara Counterterrorism Partnership (TSCTP) and the Partnership for Regional East Africa Counterterrorism program (PREACT).

One authority that is designated for the counterterrorism mission is Public Law 108-375, Section 1208, Support of Military Operations to Combat Terrorism. Section 1208, however, is an operational rather than a SC authority. It permits U.S. SOF to train "foreign or irregular (surrogate) forces facilitating ongoing military operations by U.S. Special Forces to combat terrorism," yet it explicitly prohibits the building of partner-nation military capacity. This unique authority is therefore not appropriate for consolidation. Another well-funded statute, CTPF, introduced by Public Law 113-291, Section 1510, is focused on counterterrorism, but it allows the transfer of funds rather than providing DoD with new authority. Therefore, it would not be considered a core authority.

There does not appear to be a need to make any major changes to Section 1208 or the CTPF. Moreover, it is likely that the DoD will continue to rely on standardized activity-based authorities to provide routine counterterrorism engagements and training with foreign forces and to utilize partner-based authorities to address particular terrorist threats, thus obviating the need for new mission-based authorities.

Cooperative BMD has been an area of increasing interest over the last decade due to growing concerns over strategic missile threats in the Pacific and the Middle East. Yet DoD's authority to engage in SC with foreign partners in this highly complex mission has been limited primarily to supporting Title 22 FMS programs. Currently, there

Table 4.8
Changes to Cooperative BMD Authorities

Authority and Purpose	Suggested Change (Consolidate, Revise, Clarify, New Authority)
No existing core authority	New authority to facilitate BMD training and exercises with advanced partners, to include exercises where partner is in the lead

is only one Title 10 authority that addresses SC in the BMD area: Section 223, Ballistic Missile Defense Programs: Program Elements, which was amended by Public Law 105-85, Section 233, to include a cooperative BMD program (see Table 4.8). This statute, introduced in 1999, authorizes the SecDef to establish such a program to support technical and analytical cooperative efforts between the United States and other nations that contribute to U.S. BMD capabilities. It would not be considered a core authority, however, as it does not authorize any particular cooperative activities, such as BMD training for foreign partners, or funding for these efforts.

To address the gap that combatant commanders perceive in their ability to engage in information sharing with foreign partners and to provide training and exercises on BMD systems, Congress may consider enacting a new Title 10 BMD authority. A BMD statute could permit tailored mil-mil engagement, exercise, and train-and-equip engagements on classified systems to improve the BMD capacity and interoperability of certain advanced nations. It also could allow for DoD to participate in exercises where the United States is not in the lead, which is critical when it comes to advanced partners with which the United States operates BMD systems. Such an authority would enable DoD to improve interoperability with advanced allies in Asia, Europe, and the Middle East, and allow for greater cost sharing among advanced partners.

Maritime security is another emerging area that may face a gap in Title 10 authority (see Table 4.9). DoD officials noted that they were limited in their ability to facilitate global engagement and capacity building to improve maritime nations' management of contiguous

Table 4.9
Changes to Maritime Security Authorities

Authority and Purpose	Suggested Change (Consolidate, Revise, Clarify, New Authority)
Pub. L. 114-92, Sec. 1263—Maritime Training for Security Forces in South China Sea	Revise to enable global engagement and capacity building

waters. Congress has subsequently enacted the South China Sea Initiative that provides maritime security and maritime domain awareness assistance in the FY 2016 NDAA. This new authority provides equipment, supplies, training, and small-scale military construction for Indonesia, Malaysia, the Philippines, Thailand, and Vietnam—as well as the payment of incremental expenses for Brunei, Singapore, and Taiwan. It authorizes $50 million in funding for the initiative.

While it is too early to assess the impact of the South China Sea authority, it may be beneficial for Congress to consider expanding Section 1263 to address maritime threats in other regions, including piracy along the Somali coast and in the Gulf of Guinea, Iranian naval capabilities in the Persian Gulf, and renewed Russian interest in the Black Sea and Mediterranean. Refugee flows, particularly in the Mediterranean, are another new concern. A global authority would allow mil-mil contacts engagements and train-and-equip in maritime security to address this emerging and expanding mission area. This expanded authority would require close coordination with DoS as most maritime engagements with partners fall under peacetime capacity building in Title 22. It also may require coordination with the U.S. Department of Homeland Security and U.S. Coast Guard.

Only one existing Title 10 authority addresses the issue of *cybersecurity* (see Table 4.10). Section 1051c in U.S. Code, introduced by Public Law 112-81, Section 951, allows foreign military personnel to be assigned to DoD to obtain education and training on threats to information security. There are no statutes that specifically authorize

Table 4.10
Changes to Cybersecurity Authorities

Authority and Purpose	Suggested Change (Consolidate, Revise, Clarify, New Authority)
10 U.S.C. Sec. 1051c— Personnel Assignments for Information Security Education and Training	• Revise to allow exchange of military personnel and limited training and equipment to military and nonmilitary foreign personnel • Clarify what cyber capabilities could be shared by partner-type

the DoD to engage more broadly in information sharing and training on cybersecurity threats.

As indicated in Chapter Two, cybersecurity deserves greater focus in SC planning and implementation, and changes in statutes can help raise the priority of this emerging mission and give expression to congressional intent. It may be advisable to revise and substantially broaden the current statute to enable DoD to engage in more comprehensive cybersecurity activities with partners. The authority to assign personnel to DoD in Section 1051c could be expanded to allow for the exchange of defense personnel with foreign countries (similar to Public Law 104-201, Section 1082, and Public Law 111-84, Section 1207). This would allow DoD personnel to engage with a greater number of foreign personnel and gain a better understanding of partners' information security needs. Such exchanges would likely be restricted to certain countries with limits on the types of information that could be shared. Section 1051c also might be broadened beyond the authority to provide information security education and to include limited training and equipment for both military and nonmilitary foreign agencies. Such an authority would require Congress to clarify what specific cyber capabilities could be shared by partner-type. It also would require close monitoring and further revision as the cybersecurity mission area continues to evolve.

Partner-Based Authorities

Similar to mission-based authorities, there are a number of statutes enacted over the last decade that are tailored to a particular country or multinational organization. These specialized authorities are often intended to be of short duration and therefore remain in Public Law, although most have been extended beyond their initial date of expiration through reauthorization in subsequent legislation. Authorities designated for SC activities in Afghanistan, for example, have been reauthorized multiple times since they were first enacted. Other statutes introduced to address new security threats are in effect for only a year or two.

Afghanistan. As of FY 2016, there are at least four statutes that authorize some form of SC with Afghanistan. These include: the Afghanistan Security Forces Fund, as amended by Public Law 113-291, Section 1532, which authorizes the provision of equipment, supplies, services, training, facility and infrastructure repair, renovation, construction, and funds to Afghan forces; Public Law 111-383, Section 1216 (as amended by Public Law 113-291, Section 1232), which authorizes the use of funds for reintegration activities in Afghanistan; Public Law 111-383, Section 1217, which authorizes the establishment of a program to develop and carry out infrastructure projects in Afghanistan; and Public Law 112-239, Section 1222, which authorizes transfer of defense articles and provides defense services to Afghan military and security forces of Afghanistan (as amended by Public Law 113-291, Section 1231).

Iraq. Two authorities specifically targeted to Iraq have been enacted since the withdrawal of U.S. forces from the country in 2011. These include Public Law 112-81, Section 1215, which authorizes DoD support for the Office of Security Cooperation in Iraq (OSC-I), and Public Law 113-291, Section 1236, which establishes a new Iraq Train and Equip Fund. The OSC-I statute is limited in scope, restricting DoD activities to life support, transportation, personal security, and construction. It does not provide DoD with any core SC authorities. Rather, the Iraq Train and Equip Fund plays this role by allowing DoD to provide training, equipment, logistics, and infrastructure support to the Iraqi military and other security forces to counter ISIL.

Other partners. For partners beyond Afghanistan and Iraq, there is a series of individual authorities that address specific threats in other nations. Public Law 113-59, Section 1209, for example, provides DoD with the authority to assist the vetted Syrian opposition. Public Law 113-66, Section 1207, provides authority for military assistance to the Government of Jordan for border security operations. Public Law 113-272, Section 6, the Ukraine Freedom Support Act of 2014, provides authority for military assistance to the Government of Ukraine. Public Law 113-66, Section 1208, provides authority for support to Ugandan forces participating in operations to counter the LRA. And Public Law 113-291, Section 1253, provides the authority for limited mil-mil engagements with Burma to improve the country's military capacity to respond to humanitarian disasters. An additional statute that addresses SC but does not provide core authorization is Public Law 113-291, Section 1535, the European Reassurance Initiative, which authorizes the transfer of funding for programs, activities, and assistance to support Ukraine and other European allies and partner nations.

These and other partner-based authorities are not likely to be consolidated or significantly revised as they may be considered short-term measures. We can anticipate that the statutes regarding Afghanistan will expire upon the withdrawal of U.S. forces from the country. Authorities such as the Iraq Train and Equip Fund may be extended, but will likely end when the country reverts to using more traditional security assistance programs. Authorities to support the Syrian opposition and Ukraine will likely be maintained until the current crises resolve. And special programs designed to support foreign forces in Jordan, Uganda, and Europe may transition to rely on more standardized activity-based authorities when SC activities have been normalized.

Conclusions

Our review of Title 10 authorities indicates that there are areas where changes can be made to reduce overlap, fill gaps, and address the challenges faced by DoD SC personnel in utilizing the current patchwork of Title 10 SC statutes. The most significant muscle movements, in terms of consolidation and revision, could be made to those statutes that fall within the category of standardized, activity-based authorities, which involve routine interactions with foreign forces. For the mission-based category, it could be beneficial to consolidate or introduce new authorities, whereas for partner-based authorities, it may not be necessary to change any existing authorities, but rather to allow them to expire or to transition to routine authorities once their immediate requirements are met.

The changes that we propose for activity-based authorities include the clarification of the intended source of funding and purpose of mil-mil engagements authorized by Section 168, as well as the consolidation of regional cooperation authorities with statutes authorizing the payment of personal expenses for developing countries. These changes, combined with the relaxation of the metrics for determining eligibility of developing countries, could serve to increase the utility of mil-mil authorities and allow for more consistency of U.S. engagements in priority regions and across CCMDs.

Similarly, for exercise activities, a relaxation of eligibility requirements for the payment of expenses for participation in combined exercises under Section 2010 and possible consolidation with Section 1203 training could expand the utility of existing exercise authorities. For routine education and technical authorities, we suggest the consolidation of several statutes that contain nearly identical language authorizing the attendance of foreign personnel in U.S. military academies and exchanges to reduce the number of statutes and the bureaucracy involved in DoD's administration of educational authorities, and that one existing educational program, the CTFP, be revised to allow for expansion into emerging threats.

We suggest several revisions to the new 2282 authority in the subcategory of unit train-and-equip activities that could improve its utility by allowing for more flexible timelines and the training of multinational organizations by assimilating some aspects of GSCF, which could be allowed to expire.

For equipping and logistics activities, we recommend the consolidation of the statute that provides logistical support specifically for coalition forces supporting operations in Afghanistan with the global lift and sustain authority. Yet the more complex authorities regarding acquisition and cross-servicing agreements are proposed for further analysis before action is taken to modify them. Likewise, we suggest that authorities that focus on RTD&E and intelligence sharing activities receive additional study as they contain specialized authorities, such as large, complex weapons systems being developed on a cooperative basis or imagery intelligence for foreign countries.

Among those authorities that are categorized as mission-based, we recommend limited changes. While we suggest that six existing humanitarian assistance authorities should be better aligned to facilitate coordination, we do not recommend combining the various CN statutes as the current set of authorities enable DoD to carry out its unique mission effectively. For cooperative threat reduction, Congress has introduced a new authority that appears to be addressing emerging concerns over proliferation. And for the relatively new activity of DIB, we suggest several revisions to the MODA authority that could extend its applicability over a wider range of military functions. It is only in the mission area of BMD where there might be a need for new authority to address complex SC arrangements. For other missions, such as maritime and cybersecurity, we suggest expanding proposed or current authorities—the South China Sea maritime authority and the Section 1050c authority regarding information exchange, respectively—to better address these emerging areas.

We do not recommend any changes to the existing partner-based statutes, which are intended to be short-term measures to address U.S. security concerns in a particular country or group of countries. However, consideration should be given to migrating the activities associated with these authorities to other categories of standardized activities once near-term U.S. objectives are achieved, motivating circumstances have changed, or SC activities have been normalized.

One area that we did not address is reporting and justification requirements that cut across all categories of SC authorities. While the recent biennial reporting authority, Public Law 113-291, calls for improved country-level reporting on a number of programs, more could be done to ensure that reporting, justifications, and measures of effectiveness are aligned to ensure that appropriate monitoring and oversight is provided without creating an unnecessary bureaucratic burden on DoD, DoS, or Congress.

A revised, categorized list of Title 10 authorities in Appendix B summarizes our recommended changes in all four categories of SC statutes and the impact these changes could have on U.S. Code and Public Law. These suggested changes should be considered notional at this time, however. We do not consider the complications involved in consolidating authorities with various limitations, funding sources, and reporting requirements; nor do we explore the legal implications of revising or expanding existing authorities or introducing new statutes into Public Law. A thorough legal analysis should be required before introducing a new authorities structure into legislation. Furthermore, we did not address differences in policy oversight or managers of different authorities and the impact on DoD institutional processes. Finally, our suggested changes and overarching framework can serve as a vehicle for joint review by the Departments of State and Defense in the context of Presidential Policy Directive 23.

Our recommendations are intended to serve as a basis for further discussion among Congress, DoD, and DoS in determining how current Title 10 authorities might be streamlined to enhance their utility and to improve the effectiveness of DoD SC activities. Additional analysis will be required to uncover the details of some of the complex statutes that were beyond the scope of our study (such as ACSAs and RTD&E) and explore the full legal implications that consolidation, revision, and introduction of new authorities entails. These analyses should help to further inform ongoing stakeholder discussions.

CHAPTER FIVE

Conclusion

The patchwork of Title 10 SC authorities that has evolved over more than a decade has provided the U.S. military with multiple tools for engaging with and building the capacity of foreign partners willing to join the United States in the pursuit of common national security interests. DoD SC personnel have applied them effectively to achieve country and theater objectives in a timely fashion.

However, in seeking to provide the means to engage partners to meet quickly evolving threats, an expanding and unstructured catalog of complex Title 10 statutes—all with their own processes, funding streams, reporting requirements, and constraints—has created major challenges for these stakeholders and made delivery of SC to U.S. partners unwieldy. Growth of this patchwork of authorities has motivated a debate in the DoD and Congress over whether and how to reform it.

We view this report as providing research-based input into this debate and a way forward for DoD, DoS, and congressional consideration. It is by no means the final word on the issue, but it offers a conceptualization of how the patchwork can be streamlined to meet challenges expressed by those who must employ it and begins to take on the difficult task of reframing and revising. There is certainly more to do to ensure that changes to Title 10 authorities maximize their utility to DoD stakeholders, support the requirements of Presidential Policy Directive 23, and meet the intent of Congress. The web of legal complexities and vested institutional interests that surround Title 10 authorities will take considerable time and effort to properly untangle.

Our categorization scheme and changes to the Title 10 authorities are aimed at reducing some of the complexity, unpredictability, and gaps in DoD's SC enterprise while heeding congressional concerns. First, the categorization scheme can help structure the consolidation and revision of authorities and bridging of gaps, and should make it easier for SC personnel in the field to identify and use the authorities to plan and execute SC activities. We recommend that DoD track authorities in this framework as they are enacted, revised, amended, and repealed in the U.S. Code and Public Law to help inform planners in the field, enable more systematic legislative proposals, and structure any efforts to review and overhaul internal processes. This can support an OSD proposal unfolding at the time of writing requesting that Congress create a separate chapter of Title 10 of the U.S. Code in which to house SC authorities.

Second, consolidating and revising some of the prevalent activity-based statutes helps minimize the requirement for SC personnel to "cobble together" multiple authorities and programs for individual events or initiatives, and as a corollary benefit may ease staffing needs and reduce variation in legal interpretation. It also combines some geographically oriented authorities to make them more evenly available to all CCMDs and helps them plan across CCMD boundaries. Finally, some of the revisions and clarifications will help improve interactions with less well-endowed partner nations and with appropriate security agencies.

Third, changes we recommend should enhance predictability, ease the obligation of funding, and align funding with the provision of training and equipment to partners. Extension of funding to two years for mil-mil authorities and three years for train-and-equip statutes, as well as relaxation of obligation timelines, should improve the ability of the SC workforce to plan and implement initiatives. Moderately extending timelines can help take some of the "guesswork" out of SC planning while continuing to facilitate close congressional oversight of DoD activities. At the same time, it is noteworthy that revisions to cross FYs with obligation authority are likely to elicit resistance from congressional appropriators. And, importantly, some of the challenge of unpredictability derives from internal DoD processes and structures and DoD-DoS institutional challenges that cannot be "legislated away."

Fourth, revisions and new authorities we suggest should provide greater flexibility to address emerging threats and to bridge some gaps in allowed activities. Issues like cybersecurity, maritime security, and countering hybrid warfare are gaining in prominence as topics of desired U.S. engagement with partners; changes that broaden the focus of DoD SC activities beyond CT will give OSD, the Joint Staff, and the CCMDs the flexibility to better support U.S. objectives in a quickly evolving security environment. In addition, raising the profile of missions, such as DIB, will enable the DoD to advise partner defense agencies to improve their organic ability to absorb and sustain the education, training, and equipping that the United States offers. As indicated, despite problems with the sustainment of U.S.-provided capabilities, DoD should seek other means of support without requesting a new authority.

There are a number of issues we do not address in this report that are important topics for further investigation. DoD and congressional responsibilities to develop and review multiple, disparate notifications and reports are a burden to both institutions (and to DoS as well), and better alignment of these requirements is warranted. Additional consolidations and revisions of existing Title 10 authorities are possible, but would require extensive consultation with legal and/or legislative experts to consolidate authorities of significant complexity, such as ACSAs, in the logistics arena. How congressional appropriations influence DoD's SC enterprise and options for improvement in related processes comprise another area of potential research. There is a need to undertake a review of DoD-DoS roles, interests, and coordination processes, along with development of a common understanding of how efforts based on Title 10 and Title 22 SC authorities can be better integrated. Finally, as stated in multiple discussions with DoD and congressional stakeholders, DoD must comprehensively evaluate its own SC enterprise, including how it is organized and its professionals trained, the processes used to translate authorities into action, and how SC activities and programs are linked to strategy.

Our analysis of the challenges DoD faces in pursuing SC with foreign partners suggests that the risks of maintaining Title 10 authorities in their existing form are high. The complexity of these authorities drives inefficiencies that can no longer be absorbed by a shrinking force of DoD planners and implementers. It creates confusion internally and with foreign partners, leading to uncertainties, canceled events, and setbacks in relationship-building and capacity-building efforts. It leads to hesitation among planners, who may then propose suboptimal activities that may prove less effective in achieving desired objectives. It impedes the linking of SC activities to resources, plans, and national security objectives. And it makes evaluating progress toward those objectives extremely challenging. Finally, gaps in existing authorities risk tying the hands of DoD staff working with foreign partners to counter emerging threats from Russia, China, North Korea, and Iran, as well as nonstate actors leveraging new capabilities or tactics. Although there is more to do to fully realize a simplified and more effective system of Title 10 authorities, the framework and analysis in this report should provide a useful step forward.

List of Existing SC Authorities

The following is an extensive list of Title 10 and other authorities and relevant Public Laws that are categorized as activity-based, mission-based, or partner-based and divided into subcategories based on their primary purpose. This list is current as of the FY 2016 NDAA. The list differentiates core authorities (in regular font) from supporting statutes (in italicized font), as described in Chapter Four. At the end of the categorized authorizations is a list of key SC programs that originate in appropriations and not authorization legislation.

Although the focus of our study is on Title 10 authorities, we include SC-related Title 22, Title 50, and Title 6 authorities in brackets at the end of each relevant subcategory of activities.

Existing Activity-Based Authorities

- *Military-to-Military Engagements*
  - U.S. Code, Title 10, Section 168, Military-To-Military Contacts and Comparable Activities[1]
  - U.S. Code, Title 10, Section 1050, Latin American Cooperation: Payment of Personnel Expenses

---

[1] Title 10, Section 166a, Combatant Commands: Funding Through the Chairman of Joint Chiefs of Staff, also authorizes mil-mil exchanges; however, it is primarily utilized for exercises and, therefore, under the following category of "Exercises."

- U.S. Code, Title 10, Section 1050a, African Cooperation: Payment of Personnel Expenses
- U.S. Code, Title 10, Section 1051, Bilateral or Regional Cooperation Programs: Payment of Personnel Expenses
- U.S. Code, Title 10, Section1051a, Liaison Officers of Certain Foreign Nations; Administrative Services and Support; Travel, Subsistence, Medical Care, and Other Personal Expenses
- Public Law 104-201, Section 1082, Exchange of Defense Personnel Between the United States and Foreign Countries
- Public Law 111-84, Section 1207, Authority for Nonreciprocal Exchanges, amended by Public Law 114-92, Section 1204, Extension of Authority for Nonreciprocal Exchanges of Defense Personnel Between the United States and Foreign Countries
- Public Law 112-239, Section 1275, U.S. Participation in Headquarters Eurocorps
- Public Law 113-291, Section 1203, Enhanced Authority for Provision of Support to Foreign Military Liaison Officers of Foreign Countries While Assigned to the Department of Defense
- [U.S. Code, Title 22, Section 2151, Congressional Findings and Declaration of Policy, U.S. Development Cooperation Policy]
- [U.S. Code, Title 22, Section 2767, Authority of President to Enter Into Cooperative Projects with Friendly Foreign Countries]
- [U.S. Code, Title 22, Section 2396g(2), Availability of Funds: Distinguished Visitor Orientation Tours]
- [Public Law 113-66, Section 1205, Authorization of National Guard State Partnership Program, as amended by Public Law 114-92, Section 1203, Redesignation, Modification, and Extension of National Guard State Partnership Program (Title 32 authority)]

- *Exercises*
  - U.S. Code, Title 10, Section 153, Chairman: Functions

- U.S. Code, Title 10, Section 166a, Combatant Commands: Funding Through the Chairman of Joint Chiefs of Staff (CCIF) (for combined exercises, military education, and training)
- U.S. Code, Title 10, Section 2010, Participation of Developing Countries in Combined Exercises: Payment of Incremental Expenses
- U.S. Code, Title 10, Section 2011, Special Operations Forces: Training with Friendly Foreign Forces
- U.S. Code, Title 10, Section 2805, Unspecified Minor Construction
- Public Law 113-66, Section 1203, Training of General Purpose Forces of the U.S. Armed Forces with Military and Other Security Forces of Friendly Foreign Countries

- *Individual Education / Technical Training*[2]
  - U.S. Code, Title 10, Section 184, Regional Centers for Security Studies
  - U.S. Code, Title 10, Chapter 905, Aviation Leadership Program
  - U.S. Code, Title 10, Section 2111b, Senior Military Colleges: Department of Defense International Student Program
  - U.S. Code, Title 10, Section 2103, Eligibility for Membership Senior Reserve Officers' Training Corps
  - U.S. Code, Title 10, Section 2114, Uniformed Services University of the Health Sciences Students: Selection; Status; Obligation
  - U.S. Code, Title 10, Section 2166, Western Hemisphere Institute for Security Cooperation
  - U.S. Code, Title 10, Section 2249c, Regional Defense Combating Terrorism Fellowship Program: Authority to Use Appropriated Funds for Costs Associated with Education and Training of Foreign Officials

---

[2] Title 10, Section 166a, Combatant Commands: Funding Through the Chairman of Joint Chiefs of Staff, also authorizes military education and training; however, it is primarily utilized for exercises and, therefore, under the category of "Exercises."

- U.S. Code, Title 10, Section 2249d, Distribution to Certain Foreign Personnel of Education and Training Materials and Information Technology to Enhance Military Interoperability with the Armed Forces
- U.S. Code, Title 10, Section 2350m, Participation in Multinational Military Centers of Excellence
- U.S. Code, Title 10, Section 4344, Foreign Cadets Attending the Military Academy
- U.S. Code, Title 10, Section 4345, Military Academy Exchange Program with Foreign Military Academies
- U.S. Code, Title 10, Section 4345a, Military Academy Foreign and Cultural Exchange Activities
- U.S. Code, Title 10, Section 6957, Foreign Midshipmen Attending the Naval Academy
- U.S. Code, Title 10, Section 6957a, Naval Academy Exchange Program with Foreign Military Academies
- U.S. Code, Title 10, Section 6957b, Naval Academy Foreign and Cultural Exchange Activities
- U.S. Code, Title 10, Section 7046, Officers of Foreign Countries: Admission to Naval Postgraduate School
- U.S. Code, Title 10, Section 7234, Submarine Safety Programs: Participation of NATO Naval Personnel
- U.S. Code, Title 10, Section 9344, Selection of Persons from Foreign Countries, Air Force Academy
- U.S. Code, Title 10, Section 9345, Exchange Program with Foreign Military Academies
- U.S. Code, Title 10, Section 9345a, Foreign and Cultural Exchange Activities
- U.S. Code, Title 10, Section 9415, Inter-American Air Forces Academy
- Public Law 113-291, Section 5530, Authorized Duration of Foreign and Cultural Exchange Activities at Military Service Academies
- Public Law 113-291, Section 1268, Inter-European Air Forces Academy

- [U.S. Code, Title 22, Section 2347, International Military Education and Training]
- [U.S. Code, Title 22, Section 2347c, Exchange Training: Reciprocity Agreement]
- [U.S. Code, Title 22, Section 8422a, Authorization of Assistance: International Military Education and Training]
- [U.S. Code, Title 32, National Guard]

- *Unit Train And Equip*
  - U.S. Code, Title 10, Section 2282, Authority to Build the Capacity of Foreign Security Forces, as amended by Public Law 114-92, Section 1206, One-Year Extension of Funding Limitations for Authority to Build the Capacity of Foreign Security Forces; Public Law 112-81, Section 1207, Global Security Contingency Fund, as amended by Public Law 113-291, Section 1201
  - U.S. Code, Title 10, Section 408(C), Equipment and Training of Foreign Personnel to Assist in Department of Defense Accounting for Missing United States Government Personnel
  - Public Law 110-417, Section 943, Authorization of Nonconventional Assisted Recovery Capabilities, as amended by Public Law 114-92, Section 1271, Two-Year Extension and Modification of Authorization for Nonconventional Assisted Recovery Capabilities
  - [U.S. Code, Title 22, Section 2349aa-10, Antiterrorism Assistance]
  - [U.S. Code, Title 22, Section 8422b, Authorization of Assistance: Foreign Military Financing Program]

- *Equipment and Logistics Support*
  - U.S. Code, Title 10, Section 127d, Allied Forces Participating in Combined Operations: Authority to Provide Logistic Support, Supplies, and Services (Global Lift and Sustain)
  - *U.S. Code, Title 10, Section 2249e, Prohibition on Use of Funds for Assistance to Units of Foreign Security Forces That Have Committed a Gross Violation of Human Rights*

- U.S. Code, Title 10, Section 2341, Authority to Acquire Logistic Support, Supplies, and Services for Elements of the Armed Forces Deployed outside the United States
- U.S. Code, Title 10, Section 2342, Cross-servicing Agreements
- U.S. Code, Title 10, Section 2350c, Cooperative Military Airlift Agreements: Allied Countries
- U.S. Code, Title 10, Section 2350d, Cooperative Logistic Support Agreements: NATO Countries
- U.S. Code, Title 10, Section 2350f, Procurement of Communications Support and Related Supplies and Services
- U.S. Code, Title 10, Section 2539b, Availability of Samples, Drawings, Information, Equipment, Materials, and certain services
- *U.S. Code, Title 10, Section 2562, Limitation on Use of Excess Construction or Fire Equipment From Department of Defense Stocks In Foreign Assistance or Military Sales Programs* [3]
- U.S. Code, Title 10, Section 2667, Leases: Non-Excess Property of Military Departments and Defense Agencies
- U.S. Code, Title 10, Section 4681, Surplus War Material: Army Sale to States and Foreign Governments
- U.S. Code, Title 10, Section 7227, Foreign Naval Vessels and Aircraft: Supplies and Services
- U.S. Code, Title 10, Section 7307, Disposals of Naval Vessels to Foreign Nations
- U.S. Code, Title 10, Section 9626, Aircraft Supplies and Services: Foreign Military or Other State Aircraft
- U.S. Code, Title 10, Section 9681, Surplus War Material: Air Force Sale to States and Foreign Governments
- Public Law 109-163, Section 1208, Reimbursement of Certain Coalition Nations for Support Provided to U.S. Military Operations, as amended by Public Law 114-92, Section 1212, Extension and Modification of Authority for Reimbursement

---

[3]   One limitation is that the "President determines that the transfer is necessary in order to respond to an emergency for which the equipment is especially suited."

of Certain Coalition Nations for Support Provided to U.S. Military Operations

- Public Law 110-252, 122 Stat. 2398, Coalition Readiness Support Program, as amended by Public Law 113-291, Section 1222
- Public Law 110-181, Section 1233, Coalition Support Fund, as amended by Public Law 113-291, Section 1222
- Public Law 110-181, Section 1234, Logistical Support for Coalition Forces Supporting Operations in Iraq and Afghanistan, as amended by Public Law 113-291, Section 1223, One-Year Extension of Logistical Support for Coalition Forces Supporting Certain United States Military Operations,[4] as amended by Public Law 114-92, Section 1201
- *Public Law 111-383, Section 1234, Report on Department of Defense Support for Coalition Operations*
- Public Law 112-239, Section 1276, Department of Defense Participation in European Program on Multilateral Exchange of Air Transportation and Air-to-Air Refueling and Other Exchange Services (ATARES)
- Public Law 113-291, Section 1207, Cross Servicing Agreements for Loan of Personnel Protection and Personnel Survivability Equipment in Coalition Operations
- Public Law 113-291, Section 1210, Provision of Logistic Support for the Conveyance of Certain Defense Articles (in Afghanistan) to Foreign Forces Training with the U.S. Armed Forces
- *Public Law 113-291, Section 1211, Biennial Report on Programs Carried Out by the Department of Defense to Provide Training, Equipment, or Other Assistance or Reimbursement to Foreign Security Forces*[5]
- *Public Law 114-92, Section 1202, Strategic Framework for Department of Defense Security Cooperation*

---

[4] Modified to cover operations in Afghanistan and Iraq.

[5] Reporting requirement for Title 10, Section 127d, as well as for 13 other statutes authorizing DoD to train, equip, assist or reimburse foreign security forces.

- Public Law 114-92, Section 1207, Authority to Provide Support to National Military Forces of Allied Countries for Counterterrorism Operations in Africa
- [U.S. Code, Title 22, Section 2761, Sales from Stocks]
- [U.S. Code, Title 22, Section 2751, Need for International Defense Cooperation and Military Export Controls]
- [U.S. Code, Title 22, Section 2762, Procurement for Cash Sales]
- [U.S. Code, Title 22, Section 2302, Utilization of Defense Articles and Defense Services]
- [U.S. Code, Title 22, Section 2318, Special Authority (Drawdown)]
- [U.S. Code, Title 22, Section 2321h, Stockpiling of Defense Articles for Foreign Countries]
- [U.S. Code, Title 22, Section 2321i, Overseas Management of Assistance and Sales Programs]
- [U.S. Code, Title 22, Section 2321j, Authority to Transfer Excess Defense Articles]
- [U.S. Code, Title 22, Section 2753, Eligibility for Defense Services or Defense Articles]
- [U.S. Code, Title 22, Section 2763, Credit Sales]
- [U.S. Code, Title 22, Section 2767, Authority of President to Enter Into Cooperative Projects with Friendly Foreign Countries]
- [U.S. Code, Title 22, Section 2769, Foreign Military Construction Sales]
- [U.S. Code, Title 22, Section 2770a, Exchange of Training and Related Support]
- [U.S. Code, Title 22, Section 2776, Reports and Certifications to Congress on Military Exports]
- [U.S. Code, Title 22, Section 2796, Leasing Authority]
- [U.S. Code, Title 22, Section 8422b, Authorization of Assistance: Foreign Military Financing Program]

- *Research, Development, Test, and Evaluation (RTD&E)*
  - U.S. Code, Title 10, Section 2350a, Cooperative Research and Development Agreements: NATO Organizations; Allied and Friendly Foreign Countries
  - U.S. Code, Title 10, Section 2350l, Cooperative Agreements for Reciprocal Use of Test Facilities: Foreign Countries and International Organizations
  - U.S. Code, Title 10, Section 2358, Research and Development Projects
  - U.S. Code, Title 10, Section 2360, Research and Development Laboratories: Contracts for Services of University Students
  - U.S. Code, Title 10, Section 2365, Global Research Watch Program
  - U.S. Code, Title 10, Section 2531, Defense Memoranda of Understanding and Related Agreements
  - [U.S. Code, Title 22, Section 2796d, Loan of Materials, Supplies, and Equipment for Research and Development Purposes]

- *Intelligence Sharing and Exchange*[6]

  - U.S. Code, Title 10, Section 443, Imagery Intelligence and Geospatial Information: Support for Foreign Countries
  - U.S. Code, Title 10, Section 454, Exchange of Mapping, Charting, and Geodetic Data with Foreign Countries, International Organizations, Nongovernmental Organizations, and Academic Institutions

---

[6] Title 10, Section 2350d, Cooperative Logistic Support Agreements: NATO Countries, and Title 10, Section 2350f, Procurement Of Communications Support And Related Supplies And Services, are listed under the category "Equipment and Logistics Support."

Existing Mission-Based Authorities

- *Humanitarian Assistance/Health*
  - U.S. Code, Title 10, Section 401, Humanitarian and Civic Assistance (HCA) Provided in Conjunction with Military Operations
  - U.S. Code, Title 10, Section 402, Transportation of Humanitarian Relief Supplies to Foreign Countries
  - U.S. Code, Title 10, Section 404, Foreign Disaster Assistance
  - U.S. Code, Title 10, Section 407, Humanitarian Demining Assistance: Authority; Limitations
  - U.S. Code, Title 10, Section 2557, Excess Nonlethal Supplies: Availability for Homeless Veteran Initiatives and Humanitarian Relief
  - U.S. Code, Title 10, Section 2561, Humanitarian Assistance
  - U.S. Code, Title 10, Section 182, Center for Excellence in Disaster Management and Humanitarian Assistance
  - U.S. Code, Title 10, Section 2649, Civilian Passengers and Commercial Cargoes: Transportation on DoD Vessels, Vehicles, and Aircraft, as amended by Public Law 111-383, Section 352, Revision to Authorities to Transportation of Civilian Passengers and Commercial Cargoes by DoD When Space Unavailable on Commercial Lines
  - *Public Law 114-92, Section 1205, Monitoring and Evaluation of Overseas Humanitarian, Disaster, and Civic Aid Programs of the Department of Defense*
  - [Public Law 108-25, United States Leadership Against HIV/ AIDS, Tuberculosis and Malaria Act of 2003 (Title 22, for the President's Emergency Program for AIDS Relief)]

- *Defense Institution Building*
  - Public Law 112-81, Section 1081, Authority for Assignment of Civilian Employees of the Department of Defense as Advisers to Foreign Ministries of Defense, as amended by Public Law 113-66, Section1094

 – Public Law 113-291, Section 1047, Inclusion of Regional Orga-
   nizations in Authority for Assignment of Civilian Employees of
   DoD Advisers to Foreign Ministries of Defense
 – Public Law 114-92, Section 1055, Authority to Provide Train-
   ing and Support To Personnel of Foreign Ministries of Defense
 – Public Law 113-291, Section 1206, Training of Security Forces
   and Associated Security Ministries of Foreign Countries to
   Promote Respect for the Rule of Law And Human Rights

- *Counternarcotics*
  – *U.S. Code, Title 10, Section 124, Detection and Monitoring of
    Illegal Drugs*
  – [U.S. Code, Title 22, Section 2291, International Narcotics
    Control]
  – Public Law 101-510, Section 1004, Support for Counterdrug
    Activities, most recently amended by Public Law 113-291, Sec-
    tion 1012, Extension and Modification of DoD Authority to
    Provide Support for Counterdrug Activities and Other Gov-
    ernmental Agencies
  – Public Law 105-85, Section 1033, Additional Support for
    Counterdrug Activities, amended by Public Law 111-84, Sec-
    tion 1014, Support for Counterdrug Activities of Certain For-
    eign Governments and Public Law 113-291, Section 1013,
    Additional Support for Counterdrug Activities of Certain
    Governments
  – Public Law 108-375, Section 1021, Use of Funds for Unified
    Counterdrug and Counterterrorism Campaign in Colom-
    bia, most recently amended by Public Law 113-291, Section
    1011, Unified Counterdrug & Counterterrorism Campaign in
    Colombia, Extension of Authority
  – Public Law 108-136, Section 1022, Authority for Joint Task
    Forces to Provide Support to Law Enforcement Agencies Con-
    ducting Counterterrorism Activities, amended by Public Law
    113-291, Section 1014, Extension of Joint Task Force to Sup-
    port Law Enforcement Agencies

- *Cooperative Threat Reduction and Nonproliferation*
  - Public Law 113-66, Section 1204, Authority to Conduct Activities to Enhance the Capability of Foreign Countries to Respond to Incidents Involving Weapons of Mass Destruction (to Respond to Syrian WMD), as amended by Public Law 114-92, Section 1273, Extension of Authorization to Conduct Activities to Enhance the Capability of Foreign Countries to Respond to Incidents Involving Weapons of Mass Destruction
  - Public Law 113-291, Section 1321, Authority to Carry Out Department of Defense Cooperative Threat Reduction Program (No Expiration)
  - [U.S. Code, Title 22, Section 5901, Demilitarization of Independent States of Former Soviet Union]
  - [U.S. Code, Title 22, Section 5952, Authority for Programs to Facilitate Cooperative Threat Reduction]
  - [U.S. Code, Title 22, Section 5853, Nonproliferation and Disarmament Activities in Independent States]
  - [U.S. Code, Title 22, Section 5854, Nonproliferation and Disarmament Fund]
  - [U.S. Code, Title 22, Section 2349bb-2a, International Nonproliferation Export Control Training]
  - [U.S. Code, Title 22, Section 2301, Nonproliferation and Export Control Assistance: Authorization of Assistance]
  - [U.S. Code, Title 50, Section 2333, International Border Security]
  - [U.S. Code, Title 50, Section 2334, Interdiction of Weapons of Mass Destruction and Related Materials: Training Program]
  - [U.S. Code, Title 50, Section 353, Matters Relating to the International Materials Protection, Control, and Accounting Program of the Department of Energy]
  - [U.S. Code, Title 50, Section 2562a, Initiative for Proliferation Prevention Program]
  - [U.S. Code, Title 50, Section 2569, Acceleration of Removal or Security of Fissile Materials, Radiological Materials, and Related Equipment at Vulnerable Sites Worldwide]

- [U.S. Code, Title 50, Section 2912, Authority to Provide Assistance to Cooperative Countries]
- [U.S. Code, Title 50, Section 3711, Authority to Carry Out Department of Defense Cooperative Threat Reduction Program]
- [Public Law 111-84, Section 3101, National Nuclear Security Administration]
- [Public Law 104-201, Section 1501b, Specification of Cooperative Threat Reduction Programs, as amended by Public Law. 113-291, Section1301, Specification of Cooperative Threat Reduction Programs]

- *Counterterrorism*
  - Public Law 108-375, Section 1208, Support of Special Operations to Combat Terrorism, as amended by Public Law 114-92, Section 1274, Modification of Authority for Support of Special Operations to Combat Terrorism[7]
  - *Public Law 113-291, Section 1510, Counterterrorism Partnership Fund*

- *Cooperative Ballistic Missile Defense*
  - *U.S. Code, Title 10, Section 223, Ballistic Missile Defense Programs: Program Elements*
  - *Public Law 105-85, Section 233, Cooperative Ballistic Missile Defense Program*
  - *Public Law 105-261, Section 233, Limitation on Funding for Cooperative Ballistic Missile Defense Programs*

- *Maritime Security*
  - [U.S. Code, Title 6, Section 945, Container Security Initiative]
  - Public Law 114-92, Section 1263, South China Sea Initiative
  - [Public Law 107-295, Maritime Transportation Security Act of 2001]

---

[7]   While 1208 has a training component, it is an operational rather than a SC authority.

- *Cybersecurity*
    - U.S. Code, Title 10, Section 1051c, Multilateral, Bilateral, or Regional Cooperation Programs: Assignments to Improve Education and Training in Information Security, Established by Public Law 112-81, Section 951, Activities to Improve Multilateral, Bilateral, and Regional Cooperation Regarding Cybersecurity

Existing Partner-Based Authorities

- Public Law 110-181, Section 1513, Afghanistan Security Forces Fund, as amended by Public Law 113-291, Section 1532
- Public Law 111-383, Section 1216, Authority to Use Funds for Reintegration Activities in Afghanistan, as amended by Public Law 113-291, Section 1232, One-Year Extension
- Public Law 111-383, Section 1217, Authority to Establish a Program to Develop and Carry Out Infrastructure Projects in Afghanistan, Public Law 113-66, Section 1215, One-Year Extension and Modification of Authority for Program to Develop and Carry Out Infrastructure Projects in Afghanistan
- Public Law 112-239, Section 1222, Authority To Transfer Defense Articles And Provide Defense Services to the Military and Security Forces of Afghanistan; as amended by Public Law 113-291, Section 1231, as amended by Public Law 114-92, Section 1215, Extension of Authority to Transfer Defense Articles and Provide Defense Services to the Military and Security Forces of Afghanistan
- *Public Law 109-163, Section 1202, Commanders' Emergency Response, as amended by Public Law 114-92, Section 1211, Extension and Modification of Commanders' Emergency Response*
- Public Law 113-291, Section 1236, Authority to Provide Assistance to Counter the Islamic State of Iraq and the Levant (Known as Iraq Train and Equip Fund), as amended by Public Law 114-92, Section 1223, Modification of Authority to Pro-

vide Assistance to Counter the Islamic State of Iraq and the Levant

– *Public Law 112-81, Section 1215, Authority to Support Operations and Activities of the Office of Security Cooperation in Iraq, as amended by Public Law 113-291, Section 1237, Extension and Modification of Authority to Support Operations and Activities of the Office of Security Cooperation in Iraq*

– Public Law 113-59, Section 1209, Authority to Provide Assistance to the Vetted Syrian Opposition, as amended by Public Law 114-92, Section 1225, Matters Relating to Support for the Vetted Syrian Opposition

– Public Law 113-66, Section 1207, Assistance to the Government of Jordan for Border Security Operations

– Public Law 113-272, Section 6, Ukraine Freedom Support Act of 2014, Increased Military Assistance for the Government of Ukraine

– Public Law 114-92, Section 1250, Ukraine Security Assistance Initiative

– Public Law 114-92, Section 1251, Training for Eastern European National Military Forces in the Course of Multilateral Exercises

– *Public Law 113-291, Section 1535, European Reassurance Initiative (Transfer of Funding for Specific Activities)*

– *Public Law 111-172, Lord's Resistance Army Disarmament and Northern Uganda Recovery Act of 2009 (amends Title 22)*

– *Public Law 113-66, Section 1206, United States Security and Assistance Strategies in Africa*

– Public Law 113-66, Section 1208, Support for Foreign Forces Participating in Counter-LRA Operations

– Public Law 113-291, Section 1253, Military-to-Military Engagement with the Government of Burma

– *Public Law 114-92, Section 1261, Strategy to Promote United States Interests in the Indo-Asia-Pacific Region*

– Public Law 114-92, Section 1279, United States–Israel Anti-Tunnel Cooperation

- [U.S. Code, Title 22, Section 2271, Central America Democracy, Peace, and Development Initiative]
- [U.S. Code, Title 22, Section 2295, Support for Economic and Democratic Development of the Independent States of the Former Soviet Union]
- [U.S. Code, Title 22, Section 8422d, Authorization of Assistance: Exchange Program Between Military And Civilian Personnel of Pakistan and Certain Other Countries]

Existing SC Programs Introduced Through Appropriations Legislation or Other Means (27 Programs)

- Africa Deployment Assistance Partnership Team
- Africa Maritime Law Enforcement Partnership
- Africa Maritime Security Initiative
- Africa Military Education Program
- African Union-led International Support Mission in the Central African Republic
- Asia Maritime Security, Public Law 113-235, Section 7043[8]
- Asia Pacific Regional Initiative, Public Law 111-118, Section 8094, amended by Public Law 113-235, Section 8087
- Caribbean Basin Security Initiative
- Central America Regional Security Initiative, Public Law 113-81
- Cooperative Biological Engagement Program
- Counterterrorism Preparedness Program
- Defense Environmental International Cooperation
- Defense Environmental International Cooperation (DEIC)
- Defense Health Programs, Public Law 113-235, Title III
- Defense Institution Reform Initiative
- Global Peace Operations Initiative, U.S. Code, Title 22, Section 2348

---

[8]   Bill authorized funds to be appropriated under INCLE, FMF, and IMET shall be available for maritime security and to promote professionalism and capabilities of naval forces, Coast Guard, and other maritime entities.

- International Counter Proliferation Program
- International Narcotics Control and Law Enforcement, U.S. Code, Title 22, Section 2291
- Missile Defense Agency
- Pacific Pathways Initiative
- Pandemic Response Program
- Partnership for Integrated Logistics Operations and Tactics
- Partnership for Regional East Africa Counterterrorism, Public Law 113-235, Section 7042
- President's Emergency Program for AIDS Relief
- Proliferation Security Initiative
- Trans-Sahara Counterterrorism Partnership, Public Law 113-235, Section 7042
- Wales Initiative Fund (formerly Warsaw Initiative Fund)

List of Revised Authorities

The following is a revised list of Title 10 SC authorities that incorporates all of the proposed changes to existing authorities provided in Appendix A.

It follows the same categorization of authorities in Appendix A (as explained in Chapter Three) and reflects the consolidation and revision of authorities introduced in Chapter Four. Authorities in bold refer to changes we propose in that chapter; those that may require new designations in Title 10 or Public Law are denoted with "xxxx." This list is current as of the FY 2016 NDAA. For the sake of clarity, this list does not include related SC authorities in other U.S. Code Titles or SC programs that have been introduced in appropriations legislation.

Activity-Based Authorities

- *Military-to-Military Engagements*[1]
  - **U.S. Code, Title 10, Section 168, Military-to-Military Contacts and Comparable Activities**; *clarified and revised*
  - **U.S. Code, Title 10, Section xxxx, Global Authority for Payment of Personnel Expenses**; *revised and consolidated* (Sections 1050, 1050a, 1051, 1051a)

---

[1] Title 10, Section 166a, Combatant Commands: Funding Through the Chairman of Joint Chiefs of Staff, also authorizes mil-mil exchanges; however, it is primarily utilized for exercises and therefore under the category of "Exercises."

- **Public Law xxx-xxx, Section xxxx, Exchange of Defense Personnel Between the U.S. and Foreign Countries** (Reciprocal and Nonreciprocal); *revised and consolidated* (Public Law 104-201, Section 1082, and Public Law 111-84, Section 1207)
- Public Law 112-239, Section 1275, U.S. Participation in Eurocorps Headquarters

- *Exercises*
  - U.S. Code, Title 10, Section 153, Chairman: Functions
  - U.S. Code, Title 10, Section 166a, Combatant Commands: Funding Through the Chairman of Joint Chiefs of Staff
  - **U.S. Code, Title 10, Section 2010, Support for Partner-Nation Participation in Combined Exercises and Training**; *revised and consolidated (Section 2010 with Public Law 113-66, Section 1203)*
  - U.S. Code, Title 10, §2011, Special Operations Forces: Training with Friendly Foreign Forces
  - U.S. Code, Title 10, Section 2805, Unspecified Minor Construction

- *Individual Education / Technical Training[2]*
  - **U.S. Code, Title 10, Section xxxx, Foreign Military Personnel Attending U.S. Military Academies**; *consolidated* (Sections 4344, 6957, and 9344)
  - **U.S. Code, Title 10, Section xxxx, Foreign and Cultural Exchange Programs at Military Service Academies**; *consolidated* (Sections 4345, 4345a, 6957a, 6957b, 9345, and 9345a; And Public Law 113-291, Section 5530)
  - U.S. Code, Title 10, Section 184, Regional Centers for Security Studies
  - **U.S. Code, Title 10, Section 2249c, Regional Defense Fellowship Program**; *revised*

---

[2]   Title 10, Section166a, Combatant Commands: Funding Through the Chairman of Joint Chiefs of Staff, also authorizes military education and training; however, it is primarily utilized for exercises and, therefore, under the category of "Exercises."

– U.S. Code, Title 10, Section 2111b, Senior Military Colleges: Department of Defense International Student Program
– U.S. Code, Title 10, Section 7046, Officers of Foreign Countries: Admission to Naval Postgraduate School
– U.S. Code, Title 10, Section 2103, Eligibility for Membership Senior Reserve Officers' Training Corps
– U.S. Code, Title 10, Section 2114, Uniformed Services University of the Health Sciences Students: Selection; Status; Obligation
– U.S. Code, Title 10, Section 2166, Western Hemisphere Institute for Security Cooperation
– U.S. Code, Title 10, Section 2249d, Distribution to Certain Foreign Personnel of Education and Training Materials and Information Technology to Enhance Military Interoperability with the Armed Forces
– U.S. Code, Title 10, Section 2350m, Participation in Multinational Military Centers of Excellence
– U.S. Code, Title 10, Section 7234, Submarine Safety Programs: Participation of NATO Naval Personnel
– U.S. Code, Title 10, Section 9415, Inter-American Air Forces Academy
– U.S. Code, Title 10, Chapter 905, Aviation Leadership Program
– Public Law 113-291, Section 1268, Inter-European Air Forces Academy

• *Unit Train and Equip*
– U.S. Code, Title 10, Section 408(c), Equipment and Training of Foreign Personnel to Assist in Department of Defense Accounting for Missing United States Government Personnel
– **U.S. Code, Title 10, Section 2282, Authority to Build the Capacity of Foreign Security Forces**; *revised*
– Public Law 112-81, Section 1207, **Global Security Contingency Fund**; *to expire in FY 2017*
– Public Law 110-417, Section 943, Authorization of Nonconventional Assisted Recovery Capabilities, as amended by Public

Law 114-92, Section 1271, Two-Year Extension and Modification of Authorization for Nonconventional Assisted Recovery Capabilities

- *Equipment and Logistics Support*
  - **U.S. Code, Title 10, Section 127d, Allied Forces Participating in Combined Operations: Authority to Provide Logistic Support, Supplies, And Services** (Global Lift and Sustain); *consolidated* (with Public Law 110-181, Section 1234)
  - Public Law 114-92, Section 1207, Authority to Provide Support to National Military Forces of Allied Countries for Counterterrorism Operations in Africa
  - Public Law 109-163, Section 1208, Reimbursement of Certain Coalition Nations for Support Provided to U.S. Military Operations
  - Public Law 110-181, Section 1233, Coalition Support Fund as Amended by Public Law 113-291, Section 1222
  - Public Law 110-252, 122 Stat. 2398, Coalition Readiness Support Program; as amended by Public Law 114-92, Section 1212, Extension and Modification of Authority for Reimbursement of Certain Coalition Nations for Support Provided to U.S. Military Operations
  - U.S. Code, Title 10, Section 2341, Authority to Acquire Logistic Support, Supplies, and Services for Elements of the Armed Forces Deployed Outside the United States
  - U.S. Code, Title 10, Section 2342, Cross-Servicing Agreements
  - U.S. Code, Title 10, Section 2350c, Cooperative Military Airlift Agreements: Allied Countries
  - U.S. Code, Title 10, Section 2350d, Cooperative Logistic Support Agreements: NATO Countries
  - U.S. Code, Title 10, Section 2350f, Procurement of Communications Support and Related Supplies and Services
  - Public Law 113-291, Section 1207, Cross-Servicing Agreements for Loan of Personnel Protection and Personnel Survivability Equipment in Coalition Operations

- Public Law 113-291, Section 1210, Provision of Logistic Support for the Conveyance of Certain Defense Articles (in Afghanistan) to Foreign Forces Training with the U.S. Armed Forces
- Public Law 112-239, Section 1276, Department Of Defense Participation in European Program on Multilateral Exchange Of Air Transport, Air-to-Air Refueling, and Other Exchange of Services (ATARES)
- U.S. Code, Title 10, Section 2539b, Availability of Samples, Drawings, Information, Equipment, Materials, and Certain Services
- *U.S. Code, Title 10, Section 2562, Limitation on Use of Excess Construction or Fire Equipment from Department of Defense Stocks in Foreign Assistance or Military Sales Programs (Limitation on the Application of Authority to Transfer Equipment[3])*
- U.S. Code, Title 10, Section 2667, Leases: Non-Excess Property of Military Departments and Defense Agencies
- U.S. Code, Title 10, Section 4681, Surplus War Material: Army Sale to States and Foreign Governments
- U.S. Code, Title 10, Section 7227, Foreign Naval Vessels and Aircraft: Supplies and Services
- U.S. Code, Title 10, Section 7307, Disposals of Naval Vessels to Foreign Nations
- U.S. Code, Title 10, Section 9626, Aircraft Supplies and Services: Foreign Military or Other State Aircraft
- U.S. Code, Title 10, Section 9681, Surplus War Material: Air Force Sale to States and Foreign Governments
- *Public Law 111-383, Section 1234, Report on Department of Defense Support for Coalition Operations*
- *U.S. Code, Title 10, Section 2249e: Prohibition on Use of Funds for Assistance to Units of Foreign Security Forces That Have Committed a Gross Violation of Human Rights*

---

[3]   One limitation is that "President determines that the transfer is necessary in order to respond to an emergency for which the equipment is especially suited."

> – *Public Law 113-291, Section 1211, Biennial Report on Programs Carried Out by the Department of Defense to Provide Training, Equipment, or Other Assistance or Reimbursement to Foreign Security Forces* [4]

- *Research, Development. Test and Evaluation (RTD&E)*
  - U.S. Code, Title 10, Section 2350a, Cooperative Research and Development Agreements: NATO Organizations; Allied and Friendly Foreign Countries
  - U.S. Code, Title 10, Section 2350l, Cooperative Agreements for Reciprocal Use of Test Facilities: Foreign Countries and International Organizations
  - U.S. Code, Title 10, Section 2358, Research and Development Projects
  - U.S. Code, Title 10, Section 2360, Research and Development Laboratories: Contracts for Services of University Students
  - U.S. Code, Title 10, Section 2365, Global Research Watch Program
  - U.S. Code, Title 10, Section 2531, Defense Memoranda of Understanding and Related Agreements

- *Intelligence Sharing/Exchange*[5]
  - U.S. Code, Title 10, Section 421, Funds for Foreign Cryptologic Support
  - U.S. Code, Title 10, Section 443, Imagery Intelligence and Geospatial Information: Support for Foreign Countries
  - U.S. Code, Title 10, Section 454, Exchange of Mapping, Charting, and Geodetic Data with Foreign Countries, International Organizations, Nongovernmental Organizations, and Academic Institutions

---

[4] Reporting requirement for Title 10, Section 127d, as well as for 13 other statutes authorizing DoD to train, equip, assist, or reimburse foreign security forces.

[5] Title 10, Section 2350d, Cooperative Logistic Support Agreements: NATO Countries, and Title 10, Section 2350f, Procurement Of Communications Support and Related Supplies and Services, are listed under the category "Equipment and Logistics Support."

Mission-Based Authorities

- *Humanitarian Assistance/Health*
  - U.S. Code, Title 10, Section 182, Center for Excellence in Disaster Management and Humanitarian Assistance
  - **U.S. Code, Title 10, Section 401, Humanitarian and Civic Assistance (HCA) Provided in Conjunction with Military Operations**; *aligned*
  - **U.S. Code, Title 10, Section 402, Transportation of Humanitarian Relief Supplies to Foreign Countries**; *aligned*
  - **U.S. Code, Title 10, Section 404, Foreign Disaster Assistance**; *aligned*
  - **U.S. Code, Title 10, Section 407, Humanitarian Demining Assistance: Authority; Limitations**; *aligned*
  - **U.S. Code, Title 10, Section 2557, Excess Nonlethal Supplies: Availability for Homeless Veteran Initiatives and Humanitarian Relief**; *aligned*
  - **U.S. Code, Title 10, Section 2561, Humanitarian Assistance**; *aligned*
  - U.S. Code, Title 10, Section 2649, Civilian Passengers and Commercial Cargoes: Transportation on DoD Vessels, Vehicles, and Aircraft, as amended by Public Law 111-383, Section 352, Revision to Authorities to Transportation of Civilian Passengers and Commercial Cargoes by DoD When Space Unavailable on Commercial Lines
  - *Public Law 114-92 Section 1205, Monitoring and Evaluation of Overseas Humanitarian, Disaster, and Civic Aid Programs of the Department of Defense*

- *Defense Institution Building*
  - **Public Law 112-81, Section 1081, Authority for Assignment of Civilian or Military Personnel of the Department of Defense as Advisers to Foreign Ministries of Defense**, as amended by Public Law 113-66, Section 1094 (MODA); *revised*

- Public Law 113-291, Section 1047, Inclusion of Regional Organizations in Authority for Assignment of Civilian Employees of DoD Advisers to Foreign Ministries of Defense; *revised*
- Public Law 113-291, Section 1206, Training of Security Forces and Associated Security Ministries of Foreign Countries to Promote Respect for the Rule of Law and Human Rights
- Public Law 114-92, Section 1055, Authority to Provide Training and Support to Personnel of Foreign Ministries of Defense; *revised*

- *Counternarcotics*
  - *U.S. Code, Title 10, Section 124, Detection and Monitoring of Illegal Drugs*
  - Public Law 101-510, Section 1004, Support for Counterdrug Activities, most recently amended by Public Law 113-291, Section 1012, Extension and Modification of DoD Authority to Provide Support for Counterdrug Activities and Other Governmental Agencies
  - Public Law 105-85, Section 1033, Additional Support for Counterdrug Activities, amended by Public Law 111-84, Section 1014, Support for Counterdrug Activities of Certain Foreign Governments, and Public Law 113-291, Section 1013, Additional Support for Counterdrug Activities of Certain Governments
  - Public Law 108-375, Section 1021, Use of Funds for Unified Counterdrug and Counterterrorism Campaign in Colombia, most recently amended by Public Law 113-291, Section 1011, Unified Counterdrug & Counterterrorism Campaign in Colombia, Extension of Authority
  - Public Law 108-136, Section 1022, Authority for Joint Task Forces to Provide Support to Law Enforcement Agencies Conducting Counterterrorism Activities, amended by Public Law 113-291, Section 1014, Extension of Joint Task Force To Support Law Enforcement Agencies

- *Cooperative Threat Reduction and Nonproliferation*
  - Public Law 113-66, Section 1204, Authority to Conduct Activities to Enhance the Capability of Foreign Countries to Respond to Incidents Involving Weapons of Mass Destruction (to respond to Syrian WMD), as amended by Public Law 114-92, Section 1273, Extension of Authorization To Conduct Activities to Enhance the Capability of Foreign Countries to Respond to Incidents Involving Weapons of Mass Destruction
  - Public Law 113-291, Section 1321, Authority to Carry Out Department of Defense Cooperative Threat Reduction Program

- *Counterterrorism*
  - *Public Law 113-291, Section 1510, Counterterrorism Partnership Fund (transfer of funds)*
  - Public Law 108-375, Section 1208, Support of Special Operations to Combat Terrorism, as amended by Public Law 113-291, Section 1208, Extension & Modification of Authority for Support to Special Operations to Combat Terrorism, as amended by Public Law 114-92, Section 1274, Modification of Authority for Support of Special Operations to Combat Terrorism[6]

- *Cooperative Ballistic Missile Defense*
  - **U.S. Code, Title 10, Section xxxx Ballistic Missile Defense training with certain foreign partners**; *new authority*
  - *U.S. Code, Title 10, Section 223, Ballistic Missile Defense Programs: Program Elements*
  - *Public Law 105-85, Section 233, Cooperative Ballistic Missile Defense Program*
  - *Public Law 105-261, Section 233, Limitation on Funding for Cooperative Ballistic Missile Defense Programs*

---

[6] While Public Law 108-375, Section 1208, has a training component, it is an operational rather than a SC authority.

- *Maritime Security*
  - **Public Law 114-92, Section 1263, Global Authority to Provide Maritime Training for Security Forces**; *revised*

- *Cybersecurity*
  - U.S. Code, Title 10, Section 1051c, Assignments to Improve Education and Training in Information Security; *revised*

Partner-Based Authorities

- Public Law 110-181, Section 1513, Afghanistan Security Forces Fund, as amended by Public Law 113-291, Section 1532
- Public Law 111-383, Section 1216, Authority to Use Funds for Reintegration Activities in Afghanistan, as amended by Public Law 113-291, Section 1232, One-Year Extension
- Public Law 111-383, Section 1217, Authority to Establish a Program to Develop and Carry Out Infrastructure Projects in Afghanistan, as amended by Public Law 113-66, Section 1215, One-Year Extension and Modification of Authority for Program to Develop and Carry Out Infrastructure Projects in Afghanistan
- Public Law 112-239, Section 1222, Authority to Transfer Defense Articles and Provide Defense Services to the Military and Security Forces of Afghanistan; as amended by Public Law 113-291, Section 1231, as amended by Public Law 114-92, Section 1215, Extension of Authority to Transfer Defense Articles and Provide Defense Services to the Military and Security Forces of Afghanistan
- *Public Law 109-163, Section 1202, Commanders' Emergency Response, as amended by Public Law 114-92, Section 1211, Extension and modification of Commanders' Emergency Response*
- Public Law 113-291, Section 1236, Authority to Provide Assistance to Counter the Islamic State of Iraq and the Levant (Iraq Train and Equip Fund), as amended by Public Law 114-92,

Section 1223, Modification of Authority to Provide Assistance to Counter the Islamic State of Iraq and the Levant
- *Public Law 112-81, Section 1215, Authority to Support Operations and Activities of the Office of Security Cooperation in Iraq, as amended by Public Law 113-291, Section 1237, Extension and Modification of Authority to Support Operations and Activities of the Office of Security Cooperation in Iraq*
- Public Law 113-59, Section 1209, Authority to Provide Assistance to the Vetted Syrian Opposition
- Public Law 113-66, Section 1207, Assistance to the Government of Jordan for Border Security Operations
- Public Law 113-272, Section 6, Ukraine Freedom Support Act of 2014, Increased Military Assistance for the Government of Ukraine
- Public Law 114-92, Section 1250, Ukraine Security Assistance Initiative
- Public Law 114-92, Section 1251, Training for Eastern European National Military Forces in the Course Of Multilateral Exercises
- *Public Law 113-291, Section 1535, European Reassurance Initiative*
- *Public Law 111-172, Lord's Resistance Army Disarmament and Northern Uganda Recovery Act of 2009*
- *Public Law 113-66, Section 1206, United States Security and Assistance Strategies in Africa*
- *Public Law 114-92, Section 1261, Strategy to Promote United States Interests in the Indo-Asia-Pacific region*
- Public Law 113-66 §1208, Support for Foreign Forces participating in Counter-LRA Operations
- Public Law 113-291, Section 1253, Military-to-Military Engagement with the Government of Burma
- Public Law 114-92, Section 1279, United States-Israel Anti-Tunnel Cooperation

Abbreviations

ACSA	Acquisition and Cross-Servicing Agreement
AFRICOM	U.S. Africa Command
AOR	area of responsibility
APRI	Asia-Pacific Regional Initiative
ATARES	Air Transport, Air-to-Air Refueling and Other Exchange of Services
BMD	ballistic missile defense
BPC	build partner capacity
CCIF	Combatant Commander Initiative Fund
CCMDs	U.S. combatant commands
CENTCOM	U.S. Central Command
CN	counternarcotics
CRSP	Coalition Readiness Support Program
CSF	Coalition Support Fund
CT	counterterrorism
CTFP	Combating Terrorism Fellowship Program
CTPF	Counterterrorism Partnership Fund
DCCEP	Developing Countries Combined Exchange Program
DIB	defense institution building
DISAM	Defense Institute of Security Assistance Management

DoD	U.S. Department of Defense
DoS	U.S. Department of State
DSCA	Defense Security Cooperation Agency
EUCOM	U.S. European Command
FMF	Foreign Military Financing
FMS	Foreign Military Sales
FY	fiscal year
GPF	general purpose forces
GSCF	Global Security Contingency Fund
ISAF	International Security Assistance Force
ISIL	Islamic State of Iraq and the Levant
JCET	Joint Combined Exchange Training
LOE	line of effort
LRA	Lord's Resistance Army
mil-mil	military-to-military
MoD	ministry of defense
MODA	Ministry of Defense Advisors Program
MRAP	Mine Resistant Ambush Protected
NDAA	National Defense Authorization Act
O&M	operations and maintenance
OHDACA	Overseas Humanitarian, Disaster, and Civic Aid
OSC-I	Office of Security Cooperation in Iraq
OSD	Office of the Secretary of Defense
PACOM	U.S. Pacific Command
PREACT	Partnership for Regional East Africa Counterterrorism program
RDT&E	research, development, training, and evaluation
SC	security cooperation

SecDef	Secretary of Defense
SOCOM	U.S. Special Operations Command
SOF	special operations forces
SOUTHCOM	U.S. Southern Command
TCA	Traditional Commander's Activity
TCPs	Theater Campaign Plans
TSCTP	Trans-Sahara Counterterrorism Partnership
WMD	weapons of mass destruction

References

Contract and Fiscal Law Department, *Fiscal Law Deskbook 2014: Chapter 10, Operational Funding*, Charlottesville, Va.: The Judge Advocate General's School, U.S. Department of Defense, December 2014. As of October 13, 2015:
http://www.loc.gov/rr/frd/Military_Law/pdf/fiscal-law-deskbook_2014.pdf

Defense Institute of Security Assistance Management, *The Management of Security Cooperation (Green Book)*, Edition 34.1, August 2015. As of October 2, 2015:
http://www.disam.dsca.mil/pages/pubs/greenbook.aspx

DISAM—*See* Defense Institute of Security Assistance Management

DoD—*See* U.S. Department of Defense

Foreign Assistance Dashboard, "What Is U.S. Government Foreign Assistance," United States government, web page, undated. As of December 29, 2015:
http://beta.foreignassistance.gov

Joint Improvised-Threat Defeat Agency, *About JIDA*, web page, undated. As of October 14, 2015:
https://www.jieddo.mil/about.htm

Leary, Ryan W., "A Big Change to Limitations on 'Big T' Training: The New Authority to Conduct Security Assistance Training with Allied Forces," *The Army Lawyer*, February 2014, pp. 23–28 As of February 22, 2016:
https://www.loc.gov/rr/frd/Military_Law/pdf/02-2014.pdf

Miller, James, "DoD Policy and Responsibilities Relating to the Regional Defense Combating Terrorism Fellowship Program (CTFP)," instructional memorandum DoDI 2000.28, Office of the Under Secretary of Defense for Policy, U.S. Department of Defense, November 14, 2013. As of February 12, 2016:
http://www.dtic.mil/whs/directives/corres/pdf/200028p.pdf

Moroney, Jennifer D. P., David E. Thaler, and Joe Hogler, *Review of Security Cooperation Mechanisms Combatant Commands Utilize to Build Partner Capacity*, Santa Monica, Calif.: RAND Corporation, RR-413-OSD, 2013. As of February 22, 2016:
http://www.rand.org/pubs/research_reports/RR413.html

National Defense Authorization Act for Fiscal Year 2016, Section 1207, Authority to Provide Support to National Military Forces of Allied Countries for Counterterrorism Operations in Africa, April 13, 2015, vetoed on October 22, 2015.

National Defense Authorization Act for Fiscal Year 2016, Section 1263, South China Sea Initiative Assistance and Training, April 13, 2015, vetoed on October 22, 2015.

Public Law 112-239, National Defense Authorization Act for Fiscal Year 2013, Section 229, Regional Ballistic Missile Defense, January 2, 2013.

Public Law 112-239, National Defense Authorization Act for Fiscal Year 2013, Section 1532, Joint Improvised Explosive Device Defeat Fund, January 2, 2013.

Public Law 113-66, National Defense Authorization Act for Fiscal Year 2014, December 26, 2013.

Public Law 113-272, Ukraine Freedom Support Act of 2014, Section 6, Increased Military Assistance for the Government of Ukraine, December 18, 2014.

Public Law 113-291, Carl Levin and Howard P. "Buck" McKeon National Defense Authorization Act for Fiscal Year 2015, December 19, 2014.

Serafino, Nina M., *Global Security Contingency Fund: Summary and Issue Overview*, Washington, D.C.: Congressional Research Service, R42641, April 4, 2014. As of October 16, 2015:
https://www.fas.org/sgp/crs/row/R42641.pdf

Stuber, Michael, "Special Funding and Authorities Available to the Combatant Command," EUCOM briefing at ECCM Conference, May 3, 2011.

United States Code, Title 10, Section 127d, Logistics Support for Allies in Combined Operations (Global Lift and Sustain program). As of February 26, 2016:
http://uscode.house.gov/

———, Title 10, Section 166a, Combatant Commands: Funding Through the Chairman of the Joint Chiefs of Staff, October 28, 2009. As of February 23, 2016:
http://uscode.house.gov/

———, Title 10, Section 2011, Special Operations Forces: Training with Friendly Foreign Forces, December 31, 2011. As of February 12, 2016:
https://www.gpo.gov/fdsys/pkg/USCODE-2010-title10/html/USCODE-2010-title10-subtitleA-partIII-chap101-sec2011.htm

———, Title 10, Section 2282, Authority to Build the Capacity of Foreign Security Forces, October 15, 2015. As of February 23, 2016:
http://uscode.house.gov/

————, Title 10, Section 2350d, Cooperative Logistic Support Agreements: NATO Countries, November 25, 2015. As of February 23, 2016:
http://uscode.house.gov/

————, Title 10, Section 2350f, Procurement of Communications Support and Related Supplies and Services, December 2, 2002. As of February 23, 2016:
http://uscode.house.gov/

————, Title 10, Section 2561, Humanitarian Assistance, January 2, 2013. As of February 23, 2016:
http://uscode.house.gov/

————, Title 10, Section 2805, Unspecified Minor Construction, December 19, 2014. As of February 23, 2016:
http://uscode.house.gov/

U.S. Department of Defense, *Security Cooperation Toolkit*, Defense Institute of Security Assistance Management, accessed June 21, 2012. As of February 12, 2016:
http://www.disam.dsca.mil/pages/tools/default.aspx

U.S. Department of Defense, *Sustaining U.S. Global Leadership: Priorities for 21st Century Defense*, strategic guidance for 2012, January 2012.

The White House, "Presidential Policy Directive/PPD-23: Security Sector Assistance," Washington, D.C., April 5, 2013.

The White House, *National Security Strategy*, Washington, D.C., February 2015.

Weisgerber, Marcus, "Pentagon's IED Office Reinvents Itself for a New War," *Defense One*, July 13, 2015. As of October 14, 2015:
http://www.defenseone.com/threats/2015/07/
pentagons-ied-office-reinvents-itself-new-war/117634/